Contemporary
Machine Embroidered
QUILTS

Eileen Roche

©2004 Eileen Roche
Published by

kp books
An imprint of F+W Publications, Inc.

700 East State Street • Iola, WI 54990-0001
715-445-2214 • 888-457-2873

Our toll-free number to place an order or obtain a free catalog is 800-258-0929.

Library of Congress Catalog Number: 2004105218

ISBN: 0-87349-878-X

Edited by Nicole Gould and Candy Wiza
Designed by Marilyn McGrane

Printed in the United States of America

Acknowledgments

Over dinner at a swanky restaurant, not far from the floor of Houston's internationally known Quilt Festival, my friend Nancy Zieman gave me a gentle nudge. She said, "You should write a book on machine embroidered quilts." I was flattered and motivated to take on this project. I'm ashamed to say that it was almost a year later until the nudge became a full-fledged book proposal. But, here it is in its final form, and I am grateful to Nancy for her encouragement.

The quilts in this book were created over the course of several years. During that time, many people helped and encouraged me to learn the art of machine embroidery. First and foremost, I am grateful to Gary Gardner, CEO of Great Notions, Dallas, Texas, for his undying confidence in my ability.

I also thank: Wilma Brodeur and Joe and Gary O'Connor of Eagle Sewing Machines, Drexel Hill, Pa, for my first teaching opportunity.

My parents for teaching me to strive to be the best and enjoy the process.

My five sisters—without them I'd be a pretty boring chick.

My husband, who encouraged me from the start and often pointed out when to change direction.

My children, Janelle and Ted, who make it all worthwhile.

My friend, Mary Cooney-Sciasci, who can't stitch an inch, but can really make me laugh!

Deborah Jones, for listening to me, guiding me, and cheering me on.

Sam Solomon, creative director at Designs, for his beautiful illustrations.

Denise Holguin, managing editor at Designs, whose smile brightens our whole office.

Rita Farro and Mary Mulari for putting the Ya-Ya in new friendships.

Niki Gould, my editor at KP Books, for her patience and attention to detail. Thanks Niki, for letting my voice sound through!

Julie Stephani, acquisitions editor at KP Books, for her immediate interest in *Contemporary Machine Embroidered Quilts*.

New Amazing Designs CD!

For your convenience, and due to the retirement of certain designs, Amazing Designs has created Contemporary Machine Embroidered Quilts CD with 28 designs for the projects in this book.
The following Amazing Design numbers are now offered on one CD:
AD1004 (#44121), AD1045 (#10221), AD1091 (#89056, 89067)
AD1102 (#84082, 84083, 84084, 84086, 84087, 84088, 84090, 84091, 84092,
84093, 84094, 84095, 84096, 84097, 84098, 84099 84112, 84113
AD1157 (#58096, 58104, 98318)
AD1161 (#58275, 58278) and
Bamboo #15063
Please reference these numbers when purchasing the designs for this book.

Table of Contents

Getting

CHAPTER 1

Started

The inspiration for an embroidered

quilt may start with a collection of

embroidery designs, a favorite fabric,

or a simple idea, such as "I'd like to

make a quilt for my kitchen." No matter

how you begin, the basic idea will lead

you through the quilt-making process.

Let's take a look at the inspiration for

One Silly Frog.

This quilt began with a visit to a lily pond in an arboretum. Beautiful water lilies floated on the surface while dragonflies flitted in the summer air. I captured the moment in my mind's eye and made a quick pencil sketch.

A couple of weeks later, I spotted the bamboo batik fabric and the journey began. I searched for embroidery designs of water lilies, dragonflies, and frogs. Now it was time to transfer my thoughts into an embroidered quilt.

A spontaneous approach to designing a quilt is to use your editing software program, embroidery design templates, and fabric as your starting point, which is how I often work. This method enables me to work in actual size and create the overall design and appliqué patterns in one step.

Designing with embroidery editing software has many advantages. You can combine embroidery designs and experiment with their positions while determining the size and sequencing of embroidery designs. All editing software programs will print a template of the editing with positioning marks for perfect placement.

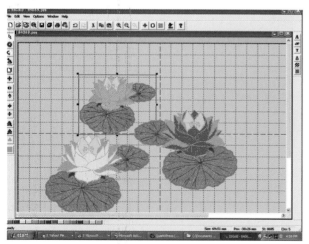

Embroidery design templates provide actual size and pattern.

Size and position easily are determined with editing software.

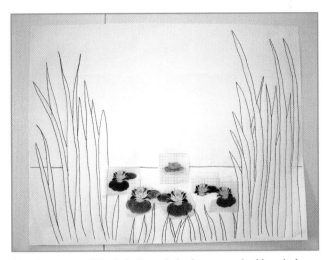

Sketch your overall block design to help size your embroidery design.

Since my focus is on embroidery, actual size is important because there are limits as to how large or small I can make my embroidery, unlike pieced blocks. If you need a 15" pieced block, you can adjust your cutting measurements to achieve that final size. If I'm making a 15" embroidered block, it will be made up of more than one embroidery design and most likely include appliqué.

With a template and fabric in hand, I'll sketch the quilt in actual size on large paper and draw any necessary appliqué patterns or decorative stitching elements.

Regardless of your approach, there are a number of tools required to complete an embroidered quilt.

Embroidery designs for quilts.

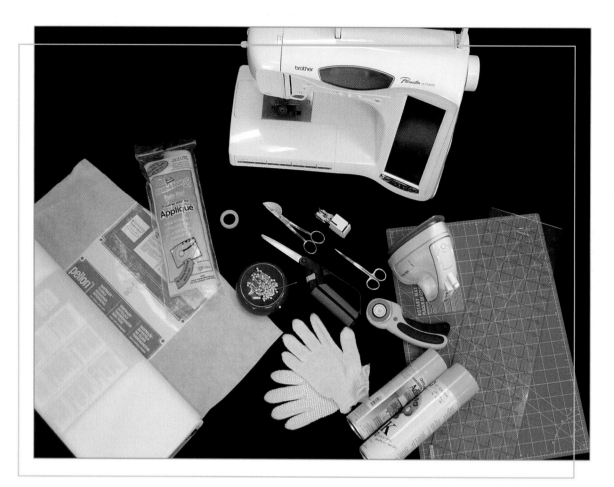

As with any quilting or embroidery project, you will need basic supplies to complete the projects in this book. Most quilters have particular brands they prefer, but all of the supplies listed can be found at your local quilt shop or online.

Basic Tools

Sewing machine
Steam iron
Thread
Needles: embroidery, sewing and quilting
Temporary spray adhesive
Fusible web (sheets and ¼" tape)

Quilting Tools

Safety pins
Walking foot
Embroidery foot
Quilters' gloves

Cutting Tools

Rotary cutter
Cutting mat
Ruler
Scissors
Appliqué scissors
Embroidery scissors

Embroidery Supplies

Embroidery machine
Embroidery editing and editing software
Hoops (multitude of sizes)
Needles
Fusible interfacing
Stabilizers: tear-away, cut-away, wash-away, adhesive
Embroidery thread
Bobbins
Peggy's Stitch Eraser
Chalk
Transparencies and tracing paper
Large paper
Tape

Fabric

As the saying goes, the fabric makes the quilt. In quilting, the fabric is the quilt; in machine embroidered quilts, the fabric is the backdrop. Keep that in mind when selecting fabrics.

Take a few translucent templates along with you to the quilt shop and audition the embroidery on the fabric. Start with a color palette, then browse the aisles for bolts in that color scheme. Select fabrics with subtle color washes, mini prints with low contrast, batiks, and hand-dyed cottons. Select a bolt and place it on a flat surface so you can see a large expanse (½ yard) of the fabric. Now, position your templates on the fabric. Close your eyes and, upon opening them, make a note of the first thing that jumps out at you. It should be the embroidery design. If it is not, the fabric will most likely dominate the overall design of the quilt.

Busy fabrics such as novelty prints, most florals, highly-contrasting paisleys, strong geometrics, and plaids are difficult, if not impossible, to embroider on. However, they often make excellent choices for borders, sashings, and cornerstones. In fact, these fabrics, when used in limited amounts can set the tone for the whole quilt.

Color washes, batiks, and hand-dyed cottons are all good choices for background fabrics.

Personally, I love hand-dyed and batik fabrics. I like the mottled effect and subtle change in color and intensity of these fabrics. Except for black, I rarely use a true solid color in my machine embroidered quilts. I think solids lend a cold, "commercial" look to machine embroidered quilts.

Thread

I use rayon machine embroidery threads for all of my machine embroidered quilts. I like the huge selection of color and the soft hand that rayon provides. Although polyester thread withstands bleaching and repeated washings, my quilts are decorative and usually hang on a wall. If they get dusty, I vacuum them. I treat them like I treat fabrics in my stash; I provide plenty of ventilation and keep them away from direct sunlight. So far, so good!

The right bobbin thread can ease the frustration of many machine embroiderers. I like to use pre-wound polyester bobbins. Consult your machine manual for the manufacturer's recommendations. Once you find a bobbin brand that works for you, stock up on them. Nothing slows you down more than winding bobbins. You'll learn nothing new from winding bobbins; treat yourself to pre-wounds, you're worth it!

Although not appropriate for a background, the black check is an excellent choice for sashings and cornerstones.

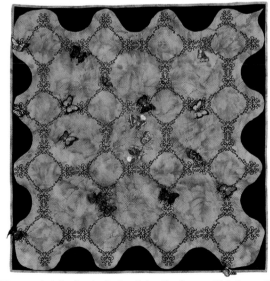

The mottled shading in the hand-dyed background fabric provides the perfect backdrop for the dainty butterflies. The black scalloped border helps to create the scene.

Understanding the basic principles of embroidery and sewing machines will result in hassle-free projects. Stabilizers back your fabric to support the embroidery stitches. With practice and time you will become experienced in what works best for your design.

Machine embroidery. For the purposes of this book, the term *machine embroidery* will refer to all computerized embroidery designs that require an embroidery hoop attached to and controlled by the embroidery machine.

Embroidery machine appliqué. A computerized embroidery design that includes adding a decorative (appliqué) fabric to the design.

Sewing machine appliqué. Decorative (appliqué) fabric is applied to the quilt with a zigzag, satin, or appliqué stitch from the sewing machine menu of regular stitches.

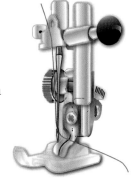

Cut-away stabilizer. A permanent stabilizer, cut-away's main function is to maintain the resolution of the embroidery design. It is available in black and white in a variety of weights.

Tear-away stabilizer. A permanent stabilizer that remains in the embroidery design once the excess is torn away. It is available in black and white, fusible and non-fusible, in a variety of weights. It should only be used when the act of tearing will not distort the fabric or the embroidery design.

Wash-away stabilizer. A temporary stabilizer that is completely removed with water. Most water-soluble stabilizers are a clear film available as adhesive or non-adhesive in a variety of weights. It is often used as a topper on knits, pile fabrics, and terry cloth. Other uses include lace embroidery, sheer fabric embroidery, and dimensional embroidery.

Heat-away stabilizer. A temporary stabilizer often used on sheer fabrics when water cannot be introduced to the fabric. Heat-away stabilizer is removed with an iron after completing all embroidery.

Template. An image of an embroidery design printed in actual size on paper, tracing paper, or transparencies with a center crosshair for placement.

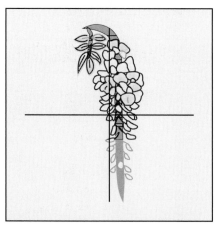

ASSUMPTIONS: You have embroidery editing software that enables you to manipulate, save, and send embroidery designs to your embroidery machine, and your machine can accommodate a sewing field of 5" x 7".

1. Backing
2. Batting
3. Pieced Top
4. Sewing Machine Appliqué
5. Embroidery Machine Appliqué
6. Embroidered Quilt Designs
7. Embroidery Designs
8. Free-motion Quilting
9. Border
10. Binding

Machine embroidered quilts are comprised of many parts. The diagram above highlights each of the components in constructing your quilt.

Basic

Techniques

You own an embroidery machine, embroidery designs, and beautiful quilting fabric. Let's explore some basic techniques that you need to know to make machine embroidered quilts.

You will need embroidery editing software with the following features:

Copy and Paste

Sizing with recalculating stitches

360-degree rotation

Mirror Image

Color Sort

View by Color

Lasso Tool

Sew Simulator

Print

Some familiar brands are Buzz Tools, Buzz Edit, Stitch Editor (Husqvarna Viking), Bernina Editor, PE-Design (Brother), Generations, Origins, Explorations (OESD), Designer's Gallery Studio (Baby Lock), Pfaff Creative Stitch Editor, Digitizer 10000 (Janome), Professional Sew Ware (Singer), Amazing Designs Smart Sizer Gold, and Size Express.

At the Computer:

1 Insert the Contemporary Machine Embroidered Quilts CD by Eileen Roche in your CD-rom drive.

2 Open your embroidery software. Go to File, Open.

Left click on File, select Open from the menu.

3 Select the CD-rom drive.

4 Select the folder with the format that is compatible with your machine.

5 Select FL1. Notice that the design name will be followed by a dot and the abbreviation of your format. Your embroidery software recognizes the dot and the abbreviation as an embroidery file. Let's look at some of the information on the screen.

- The size of the design is 39 x 140 mm. This is helpful when determining if the design will fit in the allotted space.
- The position of the design in the sewing field or hoop is also listed. The default setting is in the center,

0x0mm on the XY axis. If you move the design, the position of the design will also change.

- The stitch count is visible along with the number of color changes.
- To select the design, move the cursor onto the design and left click. Notice the design has a "box" around it with a "handle" on each corner.

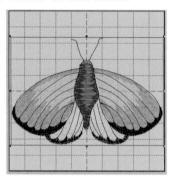

Copy and Paste: Enables you to duplicate and merge separate embroidery designs into one file. Click on the design to select it, go to File, Copy (or CTRL C) and File, Paste (or CTRL V).

Sizing: Enables you to adjust the size of an embroidery design while adding and subtracting stitches automatically. Keep in mind that the detail in an embroidery design is determined by its original size. A butterfly originally digitized at 2½" will look very simplistic when enlarged to 4½". The opposite is true, too; a highly detailed butterfly digitized at 4½" will be too "busy" at 2½".

While holding the shift key, click on the embroidery design and drag one corner handle to make the design larger or smaller. Holding the shift key will maintain the design proportions.

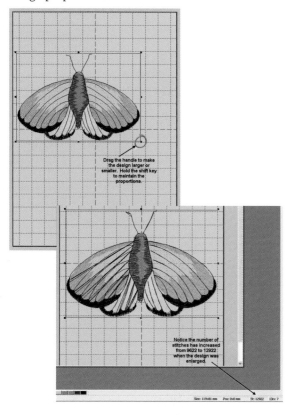

Drag the handle to make the design larger or smaller. Hold the shift key to maintain the proportions.

Notice the number of stitches has increased from 9622 to 12922 when the design was enlarged.

Size: 119x81 mm   Pos: 0x0 mm   St: 12922   Obn: 7

Rotation: Enables you to spin the design in infinite increments. Click on the rotation tool, click on the embroidery design to select it and move one corner of the design to rotate it in the desired position.

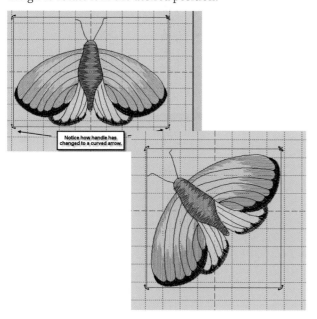

Notice how handle has changed to a curved arrow.

Mirror Image: Enables you to make an exact duplicate of the embroidery design in mirror image horizontally or vertically.

Click on the embroidery design to select it and click on the mirror image tool, (vertical or horizontal option).

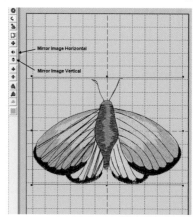

Mirror Image Horizontal

Mirror Image Vertical

Color Sort: Color sort merges all like colors into one color segment. It is especially helpful when repeating the same design in one hoop.

Copy and paste the designs into the screen in the desired positions. Click on Color Sort. This option should be used with caution as the sequencing of the color segments can be affected. Use the Sew Simulator to check for accuracy if your software program has that feature. As a rule of thumb, designs that contain the same colors and overlap may cause trouble when the Color Sort feature is used. If the designs do not overlap, Color Sort will eliminate unnecessary thread changes. Whenever you do use Color Sort, make sure you use the Save As command to avoid overriding the original design.

View by Color Feature: View By Color lets you travel

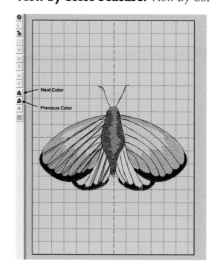

Next Color

Previous Color

through the design, color segment by color segment and lets you select, remove, or duplicate a segment. Click on the design to select it and click on the View By Color Tool. Click on the tool to travel through the design.

What is a template?

A template is a printed image of the embroidery design in actual size centered in the sewing field. The best feature about templates is there are no surprises—the location of the design is predictable and planned. Templates ensure positive and professional results in all of your embroidery projects.

Why use templates?

Templates provide perfect placement of embroidery designs. No more guesswork, the design will stitch exactly where you planned when you use templates.

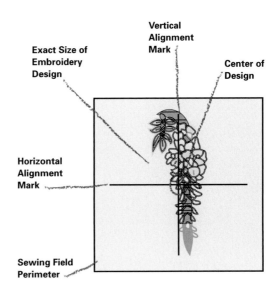

How do you use templates?

There are two areas of focus when working with embroidery designs. When designing or planning a project, the focus is on the outer edges of an embroidery design; in other words, where one design ends and the next one begins. Most of my embroidery designs will be stitched in what appears to be a continuous line of embroidery. In reality, it is not a continuous line, but rather multiple hoopings with precise placement.

The second area of focus is the center of the embroidery design just prior to hooping the item. With the template securely taped to the hooped fabric, you can see exactly where the design will stitch. Use the crosshairs on the template to square the fabric in the hoop. Place a mini-ruler in the hoop to check for accuracy.

Attach the hoop to the machine and move the needle to the center of the crosshair, using the alignment marks on the embroidery foot as a guide. Once you're satisfied with the placement, remove the template and embroider the design.

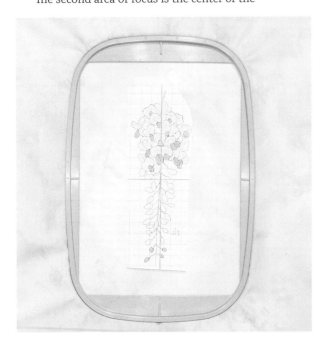

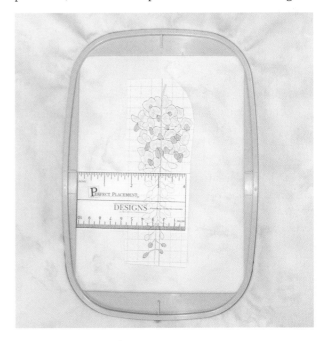

Where do you get templates?

In your embroidery software, open the desired design. Insert paper, tracing paper, or a transparency into the printer. Go to File, Print.

Paper Templates

Pros
Inexpensive
Easy to write on
Provides the actual size of the design

Cons
Opaque
Image must be cut out

Transparency Templates

Pros
Provides the actual size of embroidery design
Translucent

Cons
Expensive
Images can smear

Tracing Paper Templates

Pros
Relatively inexpensive
Provides the actual size of embroidery design
Easy to write on
Translucent

Cons
Can be difficult to feed through a printer

Manufactured Templates

Some manufacturers include embroidery templates with some collections. I designed three collections for Amazing Designs that include templates printed on vellum. Vellum is similar to tracing paper but a bit stronger; therefore, vellum templates enjoy a long lifespan.

Other embroidery collections have plastic templates that are included with the collection or available separately. Plastic templates normally have a hole for marking the centering of the design and are virtually indestructible (unless you leave them on the dashboard of an automobile on a sunny, summer day).

Tip

If the tracing paper is larger than 8½" x 11", trim the width to 8½". Tape one short edge of the tracing paper to a sheet of regular copy paper. Insert the two sheets into the printer, taped edge first, making sure the tracing paper will receive the ink.

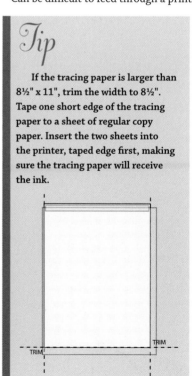

Beautiful cotton quilting fabrics are abundantly available through retail stores, consumer shows, mail order catalogs, and Web sites. They are designed to withstand a myriad of quilting techniques when coupled with a durable batting and backing. But, machine embroidery adds a whole new dimension. Quilting cottons are typically not strong enough to withstand the repetitive penetration of an embroidery machine needle and the addition of multiple layers of thread.

Selecting Your Fabric

Since we can make any fabric stronger with the use of stabilizers, choose one that will provide the perfect backdrop for your embroidery. Select solids, hand-painted muted washes, or slightly marbled cotton fabrics for best results.

Calicos, geometrics, plaids, and novelty fabrics don't work well because they "fight" for the attention of the viewer's eye. Remember, the fabric is the background. Save busy fabrics for borders, backing, and binding. They most certainly can spice up a quilt and add to a theme.

Stabilizing the Quilt Top

Once the quilt top is pieced (as in a landscape quilt), stabilize the entire block or quilt top with interfacing. Use a combination of stabilizers rather than one heavy cut-away or tear-away stabilizer.

First, fuse interfacing to the wrong side of the quilt block or quilt top. I prefer Pellon ShirTailor fusible interfacing. Once it is fused to the wrong side of quilting cotton, it eliminates the bleed-thru of any additional required stabilizers. There is nothing worse than seeing a patch of stabilizer behind an embroidery design on a light-colored fabric.

Now you can concentrate on stabilizing for the individual embroidery designs.

Recently, I've learned to love using one or more layers of polymesh cut-away stabilizer in addition to the interfacing. It is strong, lightweight, and virtually invisible in a quilt top.

Pieced Blocks

After applying the interfacing, fuse polymesh stabilizer to the wrong side of the entire block. If fusible polymesh is not available, use a temporary spray adhesive to secure the stabilizer to the wrong side of the block.

Place the block in a box, wrong side up, and spray the block with temporary adhesive.

Place the block on a flat surface, tacky side up, and finger press the polymesh stabilizer in place. If the stabilizer is too small for the block, butt the edges of the stabilizer together.

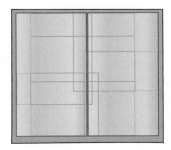

Whole Cloth Quilts (including landscapes)

Fuse the polymesh to the portion of the quilt where most of the embroidery will be located.

Stabilize the center design area.

For the other embroidery designs, hoop the quilt with polymesh stabilizer on the wrong side of the design area. Trim the excess polymesh after embroidering each design.

Use multiple layers of polymesh stabilizer when stitching very dense embroidery designs or when layering embroidery designs.

Another stabilizer to consider is tear-away which is available in different weights. Use a tear-away if you are confident the act of tearing away will not distort the embroidery design (especially ones with delicate outlines) or the quilt top.

Heavy cut-away stabilizers are not a good choice for embroidered quilts as they tend to leave a halo effect around the embroidery designs.

Many readers tell me the most challenging part of the embroidery process is hooping. If the item is not hooped properly, disappointment is waiting in the wings. And many times, you feel you did everything right. The fabric was "square" in the hoop and tight as a drum, and yet, when the item was released, puckers appeared! Yikes! What went wrong?

I'll bet that you hooped the item, tightened the screw (maybe even with a screwdriver!), tugged on the fabric for a snug fit, and stitched away. Well, it's not that simple—there's another step and an absolute DON'T to take into consideration. The extra step is setting the proper hoop tension and the DON'T is NEVER TUG ON THE FABRIC ONCE IT'S HOOPED.

Setting Proper Hoop Tension

1 Loosen the screw of the outer hoop.

2 Place the outer hoop on a flat, hard surface.

3 Place the stabilizer(s) and fabric on the outer hoop.

4 Place the inner hoop on the fabric making sure the alignment marks on both the outer and inner hoops line up.

5 Press the end opposite the screw into the outer hoop with the palm of your hand. Work both palms around the hoop until the entire inner hoop is in position.

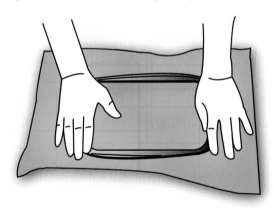

6 Tighten the screw by hand (no need for a screwdriver) until it becomes difficult to turn. DO NOT PULL ON THE FABRIC.

7 Remove the inner hoop. Now that the inner hoop is removed, the tension is evenly distributed around the entire hoop, not concentrated at the location of the screw.

Hooping

1 Lay the template of the embroidery design in the desired location on the fabric. Tape the template in position.

2 Place the inner hoop on the fabric aligning the hoop's horizontal and vertical centering marks with the crosshair on the template.

3 Pick up the fabric and hoop with both hands, holding the hoop in position. Place one end of the inner hoop into the outer hoop, hold in place, and insert the other end of the hoop. Press firmly on both ends of the hoop with the palms of your hands.

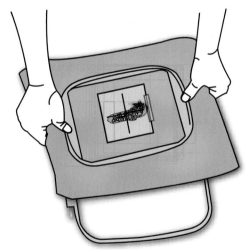

4 Gently press the inner hoop slightly deeper than the outer hoop. This technique is called countersinking and allows the fabric to sit on the machine bed and not float above the surface.

The Embroiderer's Checklist

Whether you're a veteran embroiderer or a neophyte, it's important to remember simple steps lead to successful embroidery. You can avoid frustrating mistakes by asking yourself these 12 questions before you touch the start button on your embroidery machine.

1 Is the template securely taped in the proper position? If not, the template can unknowingly move out of the desired position. Avoid this common mistake by using two pieces of tape to securely hold the template in place before hooping.

2 Is a single layer of fabric hooped with the stabilizer? As the inner hoop is forced into the outer hoop extra layers of fabric can get caught. Always flip the hoop over and check the underside.

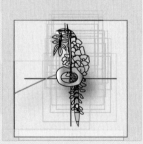

3 Are there any puckers in the hoop? Run your finger across the surface of the fabric. If the fabric snowplows, it's too loose. Don't pull on the fabric to correct the situation, instead rehoop.

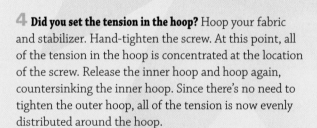

4 Did you set the tension in the hoop? Hoop your fabric and stabilizer. Hand-tighten the screw. At this point, all of the tension in the hoop is concentrated at the location of the screw. Release the inner hoop and hoop again, countersinking the inner hoop. Since there's no need to tighten the outer hoop, all of the tension is now evenly distributed around the hoop.

5 Is the fabric taut like a tambourine? Tap the palm of your hand on the wrong side of hooped fabric. It should feel tight, like a drum.

6 Does it need a topper? Many fabrics require a topper. A topper helps the stitches stay on top of the fabric and stops them from sinking into the fabric. Typical fabrics that call for a topper are terry cloth, fleece, fur, and knits. Water-soluble stabilizers such as Sulky's Solvy, Hoop-It-All's DsLV, and Dry Cover-Up help lift the threads to the surface of the fabric.

7 Have you selected the desired design from the menu? Check carefully as many designs look similar on the machine screen.

8 Does the design on the screen match the template or does it need to be mirror imaged or rotated? Make the appropriate adjustments as necessary.

9 Is the needle in the center of the template? Leave the template in position and move the needle to the center of the crosshair.

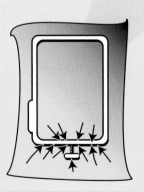

10 Is the correct thread in the needle? Check the color sequence and insert the correct thread. There is nothing worse than stitching black snow!

11 Is there anything obstructing the movement of the hoop? Clear a space on your sewing table for the hoop to move freely. Lamps, stacks of fabric, and notions can bump the frame and cause damage to your embroidery and machine.

12 Did you remember to remove the template before pressing the start button? I have lots of templates with tiny needle holes stitched in them! Although it doesn't really hurt the template, the needle most certainly doesn't like it!

Use chalk to draw a line from one embroidery design to another.

Many embroidered quilt blocks benefit from the addition of decorative stitches, mainly satin stitches. Use satin stitches to connect embroidery designs and extend the design area. With very little effort, satin stitches give a professional finish to your embroidery.

First, use chalk to draw a line from one embroidery design to another.

Set the sewing machine's zigzag stitch to 2.0mm SW and 0.35mm SL. Place the block under the presser foot, positioning the needle right into the edge of the embroidery design. Sew on the chalked line, connecting the embroidery designs.

Organizing your embroidery designs in your computer helps you access your designs quickly. Since almost all embroidery designs are labeled by number, it's difficult to remember the correct number of each individual design. This makes the locating process tedious. I have a few suggestions to help you get organized.

For purposes of this collection, it would be best to store the Contemporary Machine Embroidered Quilts CD by Eileen Roche in the sleeve provided in the back of this book. For all other collections, purchase a three-ring binder, CD and floppy disk storage sleeves, and a three-hole punch from any office supply store. Upon opening a disk collection, punch holes in the artwork (packaging and thread list if applicable). Insert the artwork in the binder and the CD or floppy into the storage sleeve. As time passes, you'll love the convenience of going to the binder and locating the exact collection.

Let me show you how I organized the hard drive on my PC creating this book.

CD-Rom Instructions

The embroidery designs featured in this book are located on the CD-Rom in the following formats: ART, DST, PES, JEF, SHV and XXX. You must have a computer with compatible embroidery software to access and use the embroidery files. Basic knowledge of your software is helpful.

Insert the Eileen Roche Contemporary Machine Embroidered Quilts CD-Rom into your CD-Rom drive. Open your embroidery software. Open and save each design in the appropriate format onto your hard drive. To embroider the designs, transfer the designs to your embroidery machine following the machine and/or software manufacturer's instructions.

Color sequences for each embroidery design are in a PDF file on the CD. You will need Adobe Acrobat Reader 5.0 or higher to view the color sequences.

To access the C drive (the hard drive), go to Start, My Computer. Open My Computer and double left click on the icon for the C drive.

Next, create a new folder and name it Embroidery Designs. Right click on any blank space on the screen, select New Folder. Type in Embroidery Designs.

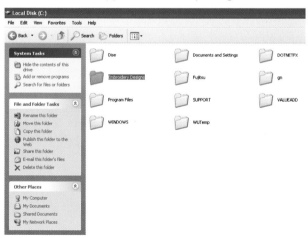

In this folder, I've created a number of categories.

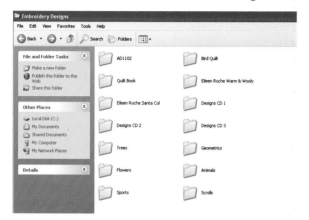

I've labeled and saved some collections by name, such as the Designs Interactive CD 1, 2 and 3. That's logical for me because they are collections that I've personally designed so it's easy to remember exactly what embroidery files are in each collection. Other files are labeled Flowers, Trees, Animals, Geometrics and so on. Each of the folders has subcategories when opened. For instance, in Animals, you'll find Cats, Dogs, Fish, Wildlife, etc. The more definitive you are, the easier it is to locate files.

Let's take a look in the Quilt Book folder. Double left click on the folder to open it.

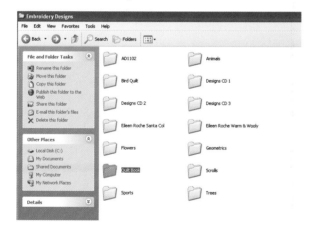

Each project in *Contemporary Machine Embroidered Quilts* is listed by name.

I've stored all of the original designs and manipulated designs that are required for that project. In doing this, some designs are in multiple locations. For example, there are three projects featuring the Wisteria designs from the Contemporary Machine Embroidered Quilts CD by Eileen Roche. Let's look in the Wisteria folder. Every design found on the quilt is in that folder.

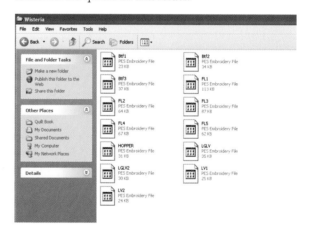

When I start a new project, I create a new folder with the project name. Then I open my embroidery software and access the designs from their original source that could be another file from the main Embroidery Design folder, CD or floppy disk. As I manipulate the designs, I save them in the new folder.

This system helps me keep track of my work as it develops. I hope you find it helpful, too!

Embroidered

CHAPTER 3

Pieced Blocks

One of the simplest ways to create a machine embroidered quilt is to piece smaller, embroidered blocks with traditional sashing or piecework blocks. Many embroidery collections are theme-based and lend themselves perfectly to theme quilts. *Oriental Images* is a great example of how to combine themed embroidery designs with novelty and solid fabrics. *Oriental Images'* simple layout, two vertical blocks split with three smaller horizontal blocks, allows the embroidery to have the spotlight.

Oriental Images

Many interior designers say every
home should have a touch of Asian
influence. Oriental Images adds a
sophisticated touch to any décor. Best of
all, you have an excuse to purchase and
use a gorgeous Oriental print.

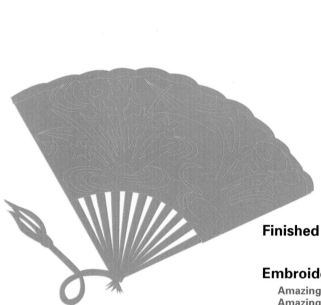

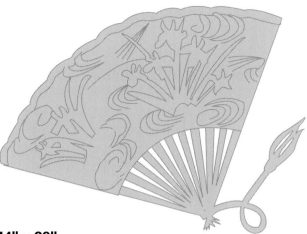

Finished size: 44" x 29"

Embroidery Collections

Amazing Designs Oriental Collection I AD1018
Amazing Designs Asian Home Decor I AD1095

Materials

Fabrics:
   1 yd. black
   1 yd. Oriental print
   ½ yd. brown hand-dyed
   47" x 30" backing
   16" x 10" black tulle
   ½ yd. binding
Batting: 47" x 30"
2 yd. Pellon ShirTailor interfacing
Polymesh stabilizer

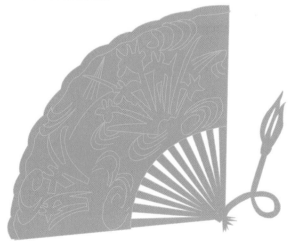

Cutting

Black:
   (2) 10" x 29"
   (2) 16" x 11"
   (1) 15" x 18"
Brown:
   (1) 16" x 11"
   (4) 1½" x 29"
Print: (4) 4" x 29"

Fuse the interfacing to the wrong side of all black blocks.

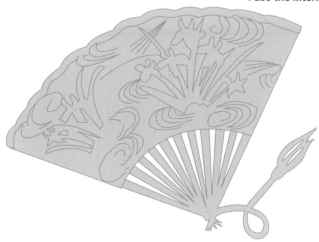

Preparing the Designs

1 Open the cherry blossom design in the embroidery software.

2 Click on the View by Color tool. Travel through the design to color segment number four and delete it.

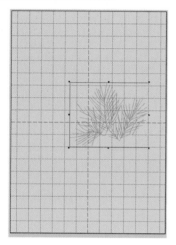

3 Save the design as Cherry Branch. Copy (CTRL C) and paste (CTRL V) the design. Mirror image the design and position it so that it connects with the first Cherry Branch.

4 If your customizing software has a color sort feature, use it now to streamline the embroidery process. Save the design as Cherry Branch 2.

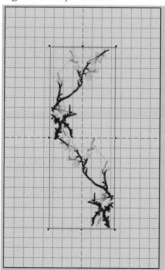

5 Place tracing paper into the printer and print two templates of Cherry Branch 2 and one template of Cherry Branch.

Preparing the Fabric

1 Place the quilt block in a deep box and spray the wrong side with temporary adhesive.

2 Place the polymesh stabilizer on the sticky surface and finger press in place.

3 Tape the templates in a vertical fashion in the center of the 10" x 29" black fabric. To make the branch appear a continuous line of embroidery, overlap the templates so that the branches connect. The best results are achieved when the newest growth (the top design) is embroidered first, so number the designs accordingly.

4 Replace the full size templates with miniature crosshairs. To make a miniature crosshair, draw a cross on a piece of tape. Write the design name on the tape. Position the miniature crosshair under the corresponding template.

Embroidering the Designs

1 Hoop the first design area, centering the crosshair in the hoop. Make sure the needle is in the center of the first crosshair. If necessary, move the hoop by touching the editing arrows on the machine screen. Embroider the design.

2 Remove the quilt block from the hoop.

3 Use an iron to remove any hoop marks.

4 Hoop the quilt block, centering the second miniature crosshair. Place the template back in the hoop, aligning the crosshair on the fabric with the template crosshair. Make sure the image on the template will connect with the embroidered design. If necessary, reposition the template. Embroider the design.

5 Repeat for the last design.

6 Place the block, wrong side up, on a pressing surface covered with a terry cloth towel and press.

7 Trim the block to 6" x 28".

Although the embroidered area of the Herons at the Pond 15" x 9½"
block is 9" x 7½", only two embroidery designs are used to create the
whole scene. The scene is built from the background (seven repeats
of the bamboo design plus extra water) to the foreground (three heron
designs).

Preparing the Designs for the Background

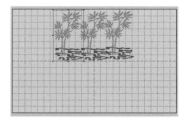

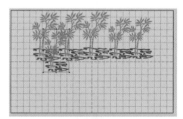

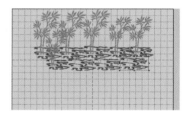

1 Open the bamboo design from the AD Contemporary Machine Embroidered Quilts CD. Select a large hoop and copy and paste the design twice. Move the three designs to the top of the hoop as illustrated.

3 Paste the small bamboo design again and move it in front of the first bamboo design.

5 Copy and paste the water three times and position each one in a horizontal line in front of the bamboo designs as illustrated.

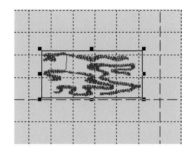

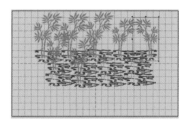

2 Paste a fourth design and decrease the size to 39.5mm x 65.4mm. Move it to the right of the larger designs. Copy, paste, and mirror image the smaller design and move it to the right as illustrated.

4 Select only the water.

6 Add another row of water and one bamboo design (#15063) to the foreground. The complete design should measure approximately 192mm x 117mm. Color sort the design and save it as Bamboo Background.

Preparing the Designs for the Foreground

1 Open the heron design #15077 and move it to the upper right portion of the hoop. Copy and paste the heron and move the design down and to the left.

2 Copy and paste the heron again. Mirror image and move the third heron to the left portion of the hoop.

3 Select the first heron (in the upper right) and decrease the size approximately 25% so that the three herons are placed in a believable composition. The design should measure 234mm x 111mm. Color sort the design and save it as 3 Herons.

4 Place tracing paper into the printer and print a template of both Bamboo Background and 3 Herons. Send the designs to the embroidery machine.

Embroidering the Designs

1 Position the Bamboo Background template on the 16" x 11" quilt block, centering it horizontally and leaving room for 3 Herons.

2 Place the 3 Herons template in the foreground.

3 Replace the templates with miniature crosshairs when satisfied with the composition.

4 Hoop the fabric and embroider Bamboo Background first. Remove the fabric from the hoop.

5 Use an iron to remove any hoop marks.

6 Check the positioning of the second design by placing the 3 Herons template on the marked crosshair. Make any necessary adjustments.

7 Hoop the quilt block, centering the second crosshair and embroider the 3 Herons design.

8 Remove the fabric from the hoop and press.

9 Trim the block to 15½" x 10".

Preparing the Designs

1 Open the bonsai design (#84067) in the customizing software. Open the geisha girl design (#15055), copy the geisha girl and paste it into the bonsai design. Move the geisha to the right of the plant.

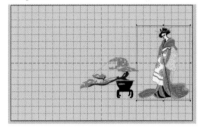

2 Paste the geisha again, mirror image the design and move it to the left of the bonsai plant. Select the bonsai design, mirror image the design and enlarge it to 84.1mm x 57.4mm. Center the bonsai design between the geisha girl designs. Save the design as Geisha Block. Print a template of the design.

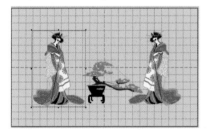

Embroidering the Designs

1 Center and tape the Geisha Block template on the 15" x 8" block.

2 Hoop the fabric, centering the crosshair.

3 Embroider the designs, using a variety of colors for the kimonos.

4 Remove the fabric from the hoop and press away any hoop marks.

5 Trace the fan shape appliqué from the pattern on pages 40-41 onto tulle.

6 Lay the tulle fan shape over the geisha block (right sides together), centering the embroidery.

7 Stitch on the traced line.

8 Trim the seam allowance to a narrow ¼".

9 Slit open the tulle and turn right-side out.

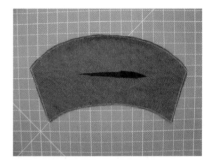

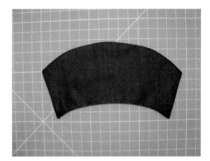

10 Press.

11 Center and pin the fan appliqué onto the 15" x 9½" rectangle of brown fabric.

12 Machine appliqué the fan onto the block using monofilament thread in the needle and an appliqué stitch.

Preparing the Designs

1 Open the cherry blossom design in customizing software. Select a large hoop and copy and paste the design twice. Move the three designs to the top of the hoop as illustrated, rotating the design on the right to create an arch.

2 Paste a fourth design under the arch connecting the branches. Color sort the design and save it as HCh Blossom. Print a template of the design.

Embroidering the Designs

1 Center and tape the HCh Blossom template on the 15" x 10" block.

2 Hoop the fabric, centering the cross-hair.

3 Embroider the design.

4 Remove the fabric from the hoop and press away any hoop marks.

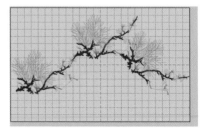

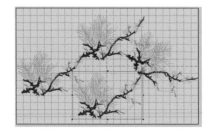

Preparing the Designs

1 Open the fan design in the customizing software. Select a large hoop. Copy and paste two fans. Stack the fans in a vertical tower. Select the fan in the middle, mirror image, and rotate it as illustrated. Save as 3Fans.

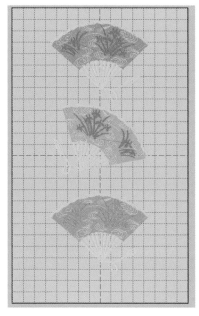

2 Open a new hoop and paste two fans, rotating one of the fans as illustrated. Save as 2Fans.

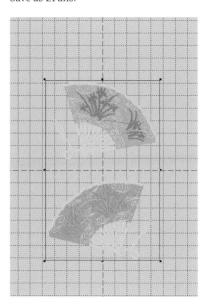

3 Print templates of the single fan design, 3Fans, and 2Fans.

Embroidering the Designs

1 Tape the templates in a vertical fashion in the center of the 10" x 29" black fabric, omitting a space under the fan at the top.

2 Replace the templates with miniature crosshairs.

3 Hoop the fabric, centering the first crosshair. Embroider the design. Remove the block from the hoop and press.

4 Repeat for all of the fan designs.

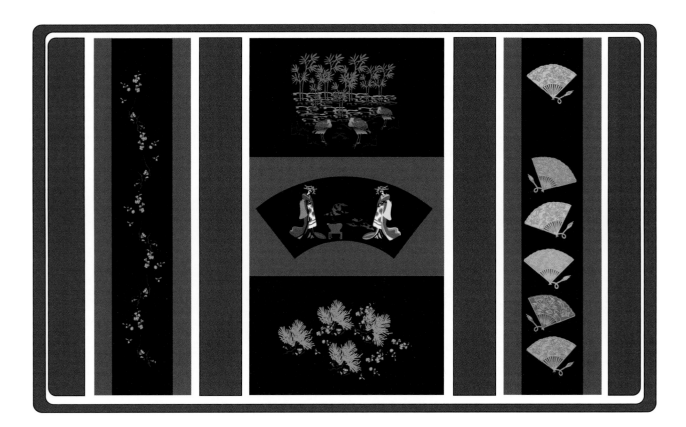

Piecing

1 Sew the three central embroidered blocks together with ¼" seam allowances.

2 Sew the brown strips and print sashings to the embroidered blocks as shown.

3 Layer the quilt top with the backing and batting.

4 Pin the layers.

5 Quilt in the ditch of all seams.

Appliquéd Banners

1 Trace the banner shapes from the pattern on page 39 onto fusible web.

2 Remove the protective paper and position the banners on the quilt. Fuse in place.

3 Satin stitch over the raw edges, (SW: 2.0; SL: .030)

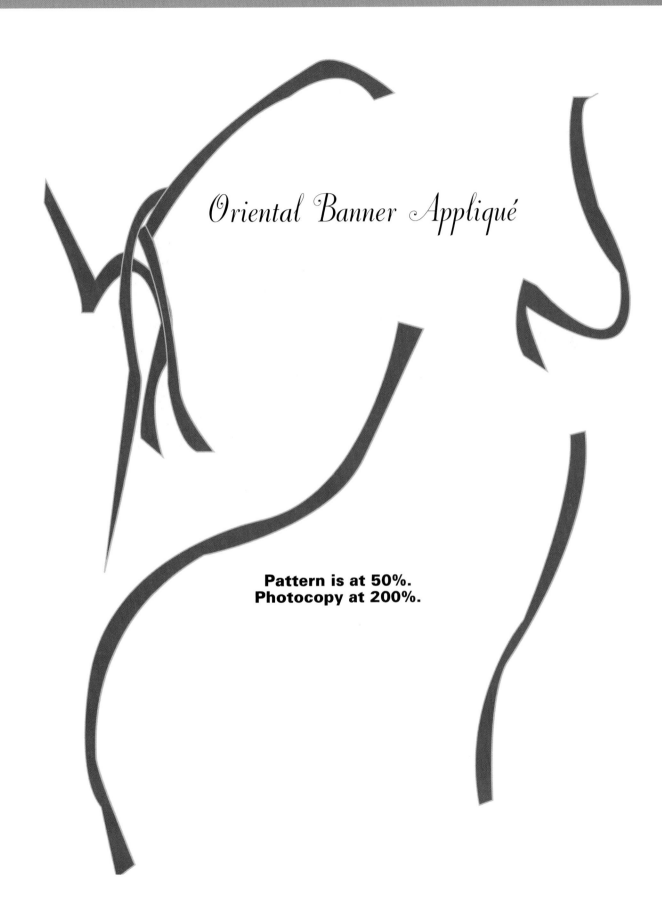

Oriental Banner Appliqué

Pattern is at 50%.
Photocopy at 200%.

Oriental Center Fan

**Copy and join pattern
at the dotted line.**

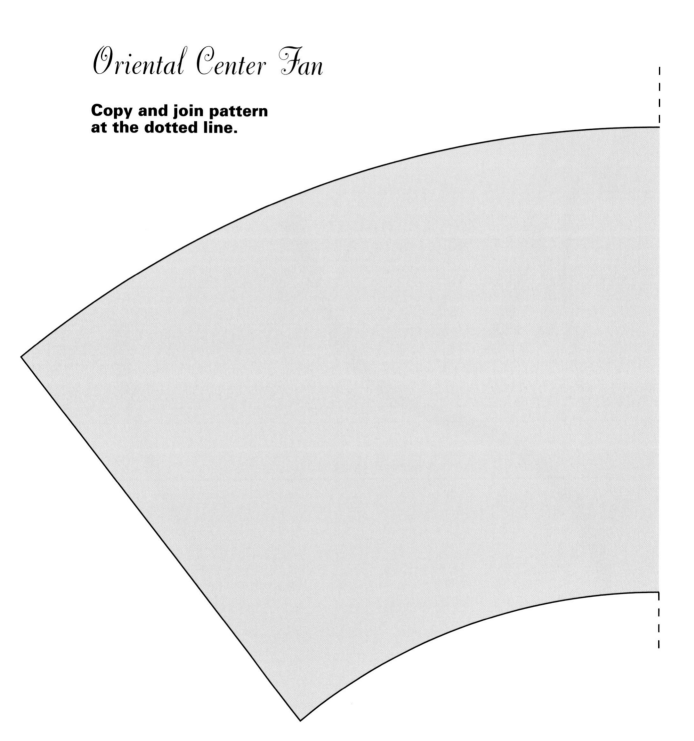

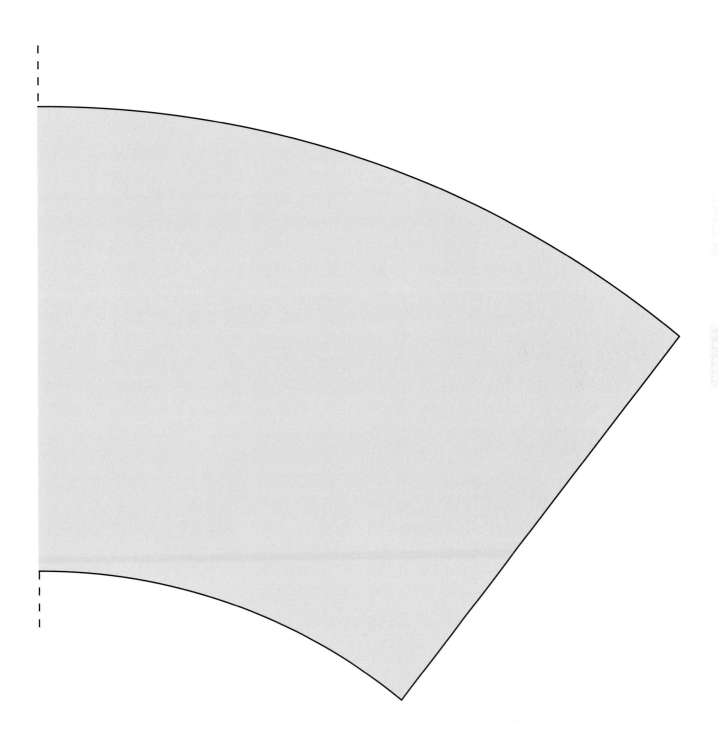

Wisteria Pillow

Try your hand at this simple project. You will
learn how to combine four embroidery designs in
your software and embroider them on an appliquéd
medallion.

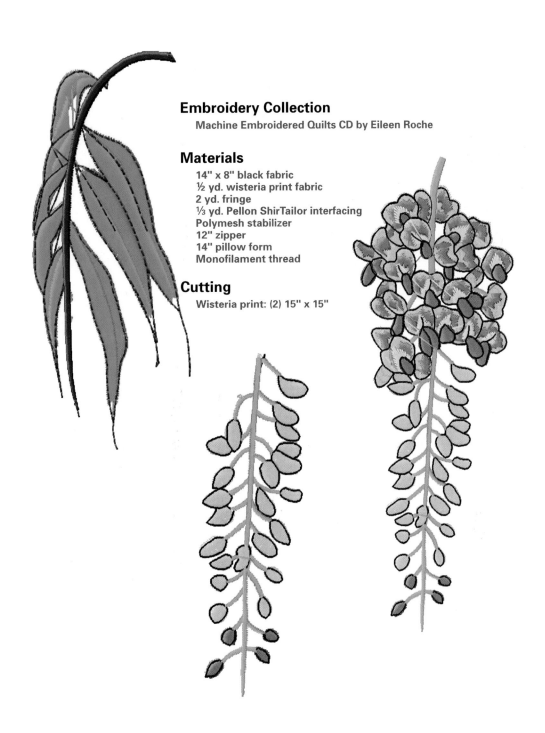

Embroidery Collection

Machine Embroidered Quilts CD by Eileen Roche

Materials

14" x 8" black fabric
½ yd. wisteria print fabric
2 yd. fringe
⅓ yd. Pellon ShirTailor interfacing
Polymesh stabilizer
12" zipper
14" pillow form
Monofilament thread

Cutting

Wisteria print: (2) 15" x 15"

Preparing the Designs

1 Open design Bud1 in customizing software.

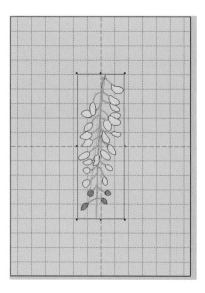

2 Open FL2. Copy (Ctrl C) the design and paste it (Ctrl V) into Bud1 as illustrated.

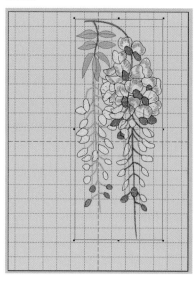

3 Open FL1. Copy (Ctrl C) the design and paste it (Ctrl V) into Bud1 as illustrated.

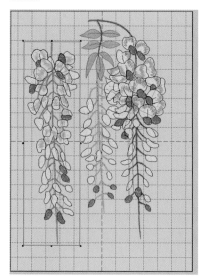

4 Open Lv1. Mirror Image and Copy (Ctrl C) the leaf.

5 Paste (Ctrl V) the leaf into Bud1 as illustrated. Save the design as Pillow.

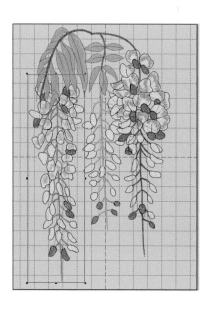

Embroidering the Designs

1 Fuse the interfacing to the wrong side of the black fabric.

2 Load the interfaced fabric and polymesh stabilizer into the hoop.

3 Embroider the design and remove the fabric from the hoop.

Appliquéing the Arch

1 Create a paper arch pattern 5" x 11". The curve starts 8" from the bottom. Center the arch pattern over the embroidery. Trace the arch.

3 Sew on the traced line.

4 Trim the excess appliqué fabric.

2 Pin the embroidered appliqué to the pillow front.

5 Add light tear-away to the wrong side of the design area and satin stitch over the raw edge of the appliqué (SW: 2.5; SL: 0.35).

Making the Pillow

1 Insert a zipper in the pillow back. Open the zipper. Set aside the pillow back.

2 Baste the fringe trim to the pillow front.

3 Pin the pillow front to the pillow back, right sides together.

4 Stitch the seams with a ½" seam allowance.

5 Turn right-side out.

6 Press.

7 Pin the decorative cord at the edge of the pillow.

8 Sew the cord to the pillow with monofilament thread.

9 Insert the pillow form.

Adding Deco

rative Stitches

Decorative stitches, such as satin stitches, are like the icing on the cake when applied to embroidery.

I use satin stitches to connect embroidery designs, fill in empty areas, and create frames because the embroidery appears "plopped" without the satin stitching. I have an aversion to what I call Plop and Drop Embroidery. Plop and Drop Embroidery occurs when embroidery designs are stitched with little thought to the final outcome. It not only looks unprofessional, but also possesses little artistic flair. As artistic sewers, we have a unique opportunity to combine computerized machine embroidery with sewing machine stitches.

Nature's Bounty

Nature's Bounty was inspired by a visit to my local grocery store on a cold, gray January day in Philadelphia. The colorful array of produce leapt out to my color-starved soul. I noticed how enticing the fruit and vegetables looked stacked in wooden crates with burlap sacks and thought about the beautiful still life it presented. The images stayed with me until I found the perfect fabrics and embroidery designs to create *Nature's Bounty*. Now this quilt is a gentle reminder of just how inspiring a cold day can be.

The beauty of nature is that nothing is perfect. Branches and twigs grow towards the sun, sometimes fighting for light with other plants. It's the twists and turns of the branches that make them so natural. Stitch your satin stitches with the same attitude. Twist and turn the block as you sew—you'll love the natural appearance of your satin stitching! (See page 51 for instructions.)

Embroidery Collection

Amazing Designs Fruits & Vegetables Collection II AD 1102

Materials

Fabrics:
  2 yd. beige fabric
  1½ yd. black and beige check fabric
  54" x 47" backing
  ²/₃ yd. binding
  Scraps of organdy or tulle
  Scraps of green fabric for leaves
Batting: 54" x 47"
2 yds. Pellon ShirTailor interfacing
Polymesh cut-away stabilizer
Lightweight tear-away stabilizer
Fabric glue stick

Cutting

Beige fabric:
  (6) 13" blocks
  (1) 9" x 27½" strip for left border
  (1) 3" x 28" strip for right border
  (1) 40" x 9" strip for bottom border
  (1) 48" x 9" top border
  (1) 9" x 3" strips (center blocks)
Black and beige check fabric:
  (4) 13" blocks
  (1) 9" block (large cornerstone)
  (4) 3¾" x 9" (center blocks)
  (2) 9" x 3" strips (right border)
  (3) 10" blocks (for triangles)
  (2) 7½" blocks (corner triangles)

Preparing the Blocks

1 Fuse Pellon ShirTailor interfacing to the wrong side of the following beige pieces:
  (6) 13" blocks
  (1) 9" x 27½" strip for left border
  (1) 3" x 28" strip for right border
  (1) 40" x 9" strip for bottom border
  (1) 48" x 9" top border

2 Add two layers of polymesh stabilizer to the wrong side of all beige pieces.

3 Fold each 13" block in half and in half again. Press the folds. Use the creases as centering marks for placing the embroidery.

Appliquéd leaves enhance three repeats of one design, the cluster of grapes, while satin stitching connects all of the elements.

Leaf Pattern

Leaf Appliqué

1 Starch and press the organdy.

2 Trace two leaf shapes onto the organdy using the appliqué pattern from page 50.

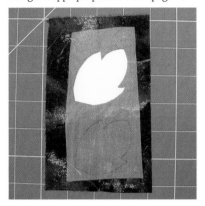

3 Pin the organdy right sides together with the leaf fabric.

4 Sew on the traced line.

5 Trim the seam allowances to a scant ⅛".

6 Slit the tulle.

7 Turn the appliqué right-side out. Use a point turner to smooth the edges.

8 Press the edges.

9 Pin the appliqués on the block.

10 Sew the appliqués in place with monofilament thread in the needle and beige thread in the bobbin. Select a narrow zigzag (SW: 1.5; SL: 2.0) or an appliqué stitch (SW: 1.5; SL: 1.5)

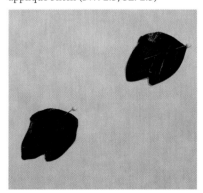

Embroidering the Designs

1 Tape template #84113, the grape design, in the center of the block.

2 Load the block and polymesh stabilizer into the hoop.

3 Embroider the design.

4 Remove the fabric from the hoop, tape the template in the second position, and rehoop.

5 Embroider the design and repeat the process for the third design.

6 Remove the excess stabilizer from the wrong side of the block.

Adding Satin Stitching

1 Press the block from the wrong side.

2 Draw the grapevine branches on the block with removable marker or chalk.

3 Place the lightweight tear-away stabilizer on the wrong side of the block.

4 Select the zigzag stitch on the sewing machine and set it for satin stitching (SW: 3.0; SL: 0.35). Sew on the line.

Six designs are placed in a pleasing, still-life arrangement in Block B. Since the embroidery designs are layered on top of each other, let's begin arranging the designs from the background to the foreground.

#84113 (green and purple grapes)

#84083 (pear)

#84090 (cut apple)

#84094 (apple and cinnamon sticks are embroidered twice)

Preparing the Designs

1 Open design #84083, the pear, in your embroidery software. Select a large hoop. Go to File, Save As and save the design as Block B.

2 Rotate the pear, click on Mirror Image Horizontal, and move it up towards the edge of the hoop.

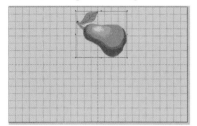

3 Open design #84113, the green grapes.

4 Copy (Ctrl C) and paste (Ctrl V) the grapes into the pear design.

5 Rotate the grapes and move them to the left of the center crosshair.

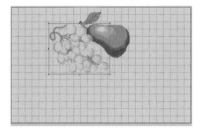

6 Open design #84094, the apple with cinnamon sticks.

7 Copy (Ctrl C) and paste (Ctrl V) the design into the pear design.

8 Move the apple with cinnamon sticks design to the lower left corner. Make sure the apple is covering a portion of the grapes.

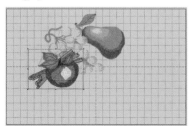

9 Open design #84090, the cut apple. Click on the Color Select tool and delete the leaf; color segments 6, 7, and 8.

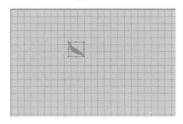

10 Center and save the design as Cut Apple.

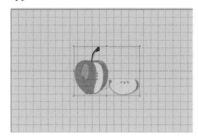

11 Move the apple over portions of the pear, grapes, and apple with cinnamon sticks. Save the design as Block B1. Print a template of the design.

12 Open design #84094, the apple with cinnamon sticks. Mirror Image the design.

13 Open #84113, the green grapes. Change the green thread colors to purple. Copy (Ctrl C) and Paste (Ctrl V) the grapes into design #84094 as illustrated. Save the design as Block B2 and print a template.

Embroidering the Designs

1 Center and tape the Block B1 template on the Block B fabric.

2 Hoop the block with two layers of polymesh stabilizer on the wrong side of the block. Embroider the design, switching to a denim needle when you get to the cut apple design. The denim needle will penetrate the previously embroidered designs without harming the embroidery.

3 Place template Block B2 on the quilt block. Center the template in the hoop and embroider the design.

If your embroidery software has a feature that removes stitches in overlapping areas, use it now. If not, embroider designs on top of designs; just use a larger needle (denim) when you get to the designs on the top layer.

It's not advisable to use the color sort feature on these designs because it's imperative that all of the colors are stitched in the appropriate sequence.

Four repeats of one design, #84088, fill Block C. The leaf from the cherry design is duplicated and added to one of the cherry designs.

#84088, cherries

Preparing the Designs

1 Open design #84088, the cherries, in embroidery software. Go to File, Save As and save the design as Block C.

2 Travel through the design to color segment #9. Using the Select Color Tool, select color segment #9, the leaf.

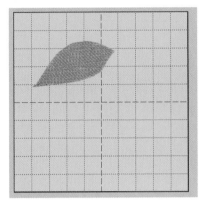

3 Copy (Ctrl C) the segment. Open a new screen (Ctrl N) and paste (Ctrl V) the segment.

4 Go back to design #84088. Advance to the next color segment, #10. Using the Select Color Tool, select color segment #10.

5 Copy (Ctrl C) the segment. Paste (Ctrl V) the segment into the new screen.

6 Click on the Select All tool and select the leaf. Click on the Auto Centering tool. Save the design as Leaf1.

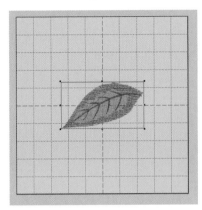

7 Go to design #84088 and copy (Ctrl C) the design. Paste the design three times in Block C. Move the designs so that they fill the hoop area. Mirror image the design on the right.

8 Copy (Ctrl C) Leaf 1 and paste it into Block C. Attach the leaf to the cherry stem on the right. Mirror image the leaf and paste it to the lower left cherry. If you have the Color Sort feature, use it now to eliminate unnecessary thread changes. Print a template of Block C.

Embroidering the Designs

1 Tape template Block C in the center of the block.

2 Load the block and polymesh stabilizer into the hoop.

3 Embroider the design.

4 Remove the excess stabilizer from the wrong side of the block.

Adding Satin Stitching

1 Press the block.

2 Draw the branches from the pattern onto the block with removable marker or chalk.

3 Place the lightweight tear-away stabilizer on the wrong side of the block.

4 Select the zigzag stitch and set it for satin stitching (SW: 3.0; SL: 0.35). Sew on the chalked lines connecting the stems and extending the lines to the edges.

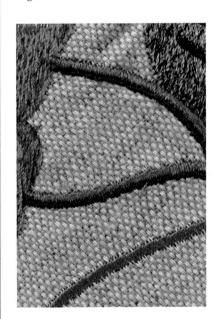

Nine vegetable designs are used to fill Block D. Since the embroidery designs are layered on top of each other, begin arranging the designs from the background to the foreground.

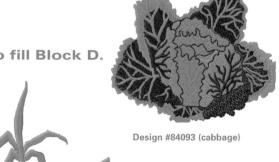

Design #84093 (cabbage)

Design #84086 (scallions are embroidered three times)

Preparing the Designs

1 Open design #84099, the carrot, in your embroidery software. Select a large hoop. Go to File, Save As and save the design as Block D1.

2 Copy (Ctrl C) and paste (Ctrl V) the carrot and mirror image it vertically. Copy (Ctrl C) and paste (Ctrl V) the design and position the carrots as illustrated below.

3 Click on the color select tool and eliminate the leaves from the carrot on the right.

4 Open design #84093, the cabbage. Copy (Ctrl C) and paste (Ctrl V) the cabbage into Block D. Position the cabbage in front of the carrots.

5 Open design #84097, the ear of corn. Copy (Ctrl C) and paste (Ctrl V) the corn and position it to the left of the carrots.

6 Copy (Ctrl C), paste (Ctrl V), and mirror image the corn. Move it to the right of the cabbage. Save the design.

7 Open design #84086, scallions. Eliminate color segments #1, 2, and 3.

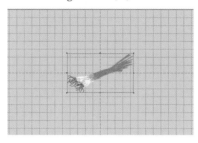

8 Copy (Ctrl C) and paste (Ctrl V) the scallions twice. Rotate and mirror image as necessary.

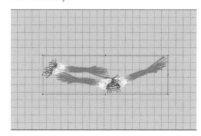

Embroidering the Designs

1 Center and tape the Block D1 template on the Block D fabric.

2 Hoop the block with two layers of polymesh stabilizer on the wrong side of the block.

3 Embroider the design. When you get to the fourth, fifth, and sixth designs, switch to a denim needle. The denim will penetrate the previously embroidered designs without harming the embroidery.

If your embroidery software has a feature that removes stitches in overlapping areas, use it now. If not, embroider designs on top of designs; just use a larger needle (denim) when you get to the designs on the top layer.

It's not advisable to use the color sort feature on this design because it's imperative that all of the colors are stitched in the appropriate sequence.

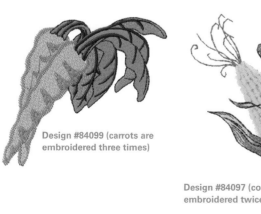

Design #84099 (carrots are embroidered three times)

Design #84097 (corn is embroidered twice)

Block E is my favorite block! I love the repetition of the single design and all of the satin stitching that connects each design. This block is not a still life as it shows movement and growth by the vines that grow right out of the block.

Preparing the Designs

1 Open design #84092. Go to File, Save As and save the design as Block E. Move the design to the left of the crosshair.

2 Copy (Ctrl C) and paste (Ctrl V) the peas. Move the design to the center above the horizontal crosshair. Select and rotate the design as illustrated.

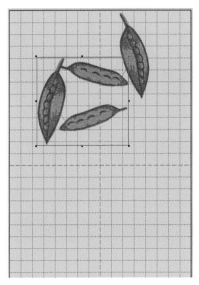

3 Paste (Ctrl V) the design and move it to the left and below the first two designs. Rotate as necessary, and save.

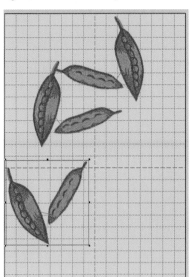

4 Copy (Ctrl C) and Paste (Ctrl V) design #84092 three times into a new screen. Position the designs as shown.

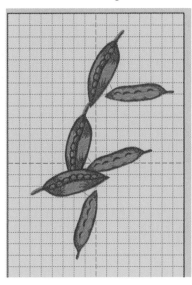

5 Save the design as Block E1. If you have the Color Sort feature, use it now to eliminate unnecessary thread changes. Print templates of Block E and Block E1.

Embroidering the Designs

1 Center and tape Block E and Block E1 templates on the Block E fabric. Replace Block E template with a miniature crosshair.

2 Center and hoop template Block E1 with two layers of polymesh stabilizer on the wrong side of the block. Embroider the design and remove the fabric from the hoop.

3 Center and hoop template Block E. Embroider the design and remove the fabric from the hoop.

Adding Satin Stitching

1 Press the block.

2 Draw the branches from the pattern onto the block with removable marker or chalk.

3 Place the lightweight tear-away stabilizer on the wrong side of the block.

4 Select the zigzag stitch and set it for satin stitching (SW: 3.0; SL: 0.35). Sew on the chalked lines connecting the stems and extending the lines to the edges.

Four vegetable designs along with some appliquéd leaves adorn Block F. Notice the variety of shapes and the balance of color in this block. Try to achieve the same results by incorporating numerous shades of green threads and appliqué fabrics.

Design #84091 (garlic cloves)

Leaf Appliqué

Freehand draw five appliqué leaves for Block F. Refer to the photo on page 60 for style and size ideas. Follow the leaf appliqué instructions on page 51.

Preparing the Designs

1 Open design #84084, the artichoke, in your embroidery software. Select a large hoop. Move the artichoke to the right of the center crosshair. Rotate as necessary. Go to File, Save As and save the design as Block F.

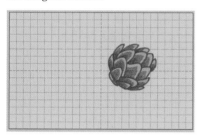

2 Open design #84095, the pepper and tomato. Select, copy (Ctrl C) and paste (Ctrl V) the design into Block F. Overlap the pepper with the artichoke.

3 Open design #84112, the eggplant. Copy (Ctrl C) and paste (Ctrl V) the design twice into Block F. Mirror image one of the eggplant designs and position it in the foreground as illustrated.

4 Open design #84091, the garlic cloves. Copy (Ctrl C) and paste (Ctrl V) the design into Block F. Save and print a template of the design.

Embroidering the Designs

1 Center and tape the Block F templates on the Block F fabric. Slide the three appliqué leaves under the template, positioning them around the artichoke. When you're satisfied with the composition, pin the leaves in place and remove the template. Appliqué the leaves onto the block.

2 Tape the Block F template on the Block F fabric. Hoop the block with two layers of polymesh stabilizer on the wrong side of the block.

3 Embroider the first nine color segments. After stitching color segment #9 (the highlight on the tomato), use a glue stick to secure the small appliqué leaf onto the tomato. Use the template to determine if segment #10 (the stem of the tomato) will catch the appliqué leaf. Continue embroidering the design.

4 Appliqué the remaining leaf between the eggplant and the tomato.

Design #84084 (artichoke)

Design #84095 (pepper and tomato)

Design #84112 (eggplant is embroidered twice)

Open design #84096, the radish, in your embroidery software. Print a template.

Embroidering the Designs

1 Fold the border strip in half horizontally. Press the fold. Use this crease as the horizontal crosshair for all of the radishes.

2 Tape the template on the border with the horizontal line of the template on the crease and vertical line of the template, 3" from the left edge.

3 Load the border and two layers of polymesh stabilizer in the hoop, centering the template. Move the needle to the center of the crosshair, remove the template and embroider the design. Remove the fabric from the hoop.

4 Tape the template on the border so that the design is 6" from the previously stitched design.

5 Embroider the design. Repeat this process for a total of eight designs.

Adding Satin Stitching

1 Press the block.

2 Draw the topsoil line with removable marker or chalk. Refer to the photo above.

3 Place the lightweight tear-away stabilizer on the wrong side of the border.

4 Select the zigzag stitch and set it for satin stitching (SW: 3.0; SL: 0.35). Sew on the chalked line connecting the radishes and extending the topsoil line to the edge.

5 Set the machine for straight stitching. Extend the roots almost to the edge of the border. No need for perfection—the more jagged, the better!

Embroidering the designs

1 Tape the templates on the border. Consider replacing the full size templates with miniature crosshairs.

2 Load the border and two layers of polymesh stabilizer into the hoop, centering one of the designs. Embroider the design and remove the fabric from the hoop.

3 Repeat for the remaining three designs.

Adding Satin Stitching

1 Press the block.

2 On the border, draw a curving line, connecting the embroidery designs with removable marker or chalk. See the photo for reference.

3 Place the lightweight tear-away stabilizer on the wrong side of the border.

4 Select the zigzag stitch and set it for satin stitching (SW: 3.0; SL: 0.35). Sew on the chalked lines connecting the designs and extending the lines to the edges.

The left vertical border has four evenly spaced designs, each connected with satin stitching. You may have already printed templates of #84088 (cherries), #84083 (pear), #84113 (grapes), and #84099 (carrots). If not, print them now. Refer to the photo for exact placement of the embroidery designs. The centers of the designs are approximately 7" apart.

Horizontal Border

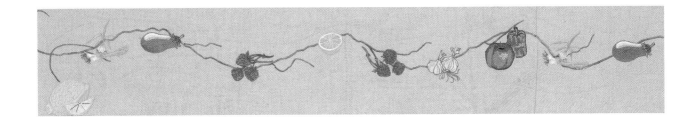

The top horizontal border has nine evenly spaced embroidery designs. You may already have some of the templates printed; if not, print all of them now. You'll need templates of designs #84098 (strawberries), #84082 (lemon), #84086 (scallions), #84087 (orange), #84091 (garlic cloves), #84112 (eggplant) and #84095 (tomato and pepper)

Embroidering the designs

Refer to the photo above for exact placement of the embroidery designs.

1 Tape the templates onto the border.

2 Load the border and two layers of polymesh stabilizer into the hoop, centering one of the designs. Embroider the design and remove the fabric from the hoop.

3 Repeat for the remaining designs.

Adding Satin Stitching

1 Press the block.

2 Draw the line connecting the patterns onto the border with removable marker or chalk.

3 Place the lightweight tear-away stabilizer on the wrong side of the border.

4 Select the zigzag stitch and set it for satin stitching (SW: 3.0; SL: 0.35). Sew on the chalked lines connecting the designs and extending the lines to the edges.

1 Piece one 9" x 3" beige strip between two 9" x 3" check strips for center blocks (G&H).

2 Add the triangles as shown in the diagram below. Sew row 1 to row 2, 2 to 3, and 3 to 4. Add the radish border.

3 Sew the 8" black and beige block to the left border.

4 Sew the left border to the quilt.

5 Add the top border.

6 Embroider the lemon using template #84082. Color sequence: yellow, old gold, yellow, old gold, black.

7 Add the right border.

8 Layer with batting and backing. Quilt as desired. Sample is stitched-in-the-ditch with outline quilting in the left and top borders (monofilament thread). The radish roots were stitched in dark brown, free-motion.

9 Bind the quilt as desired.

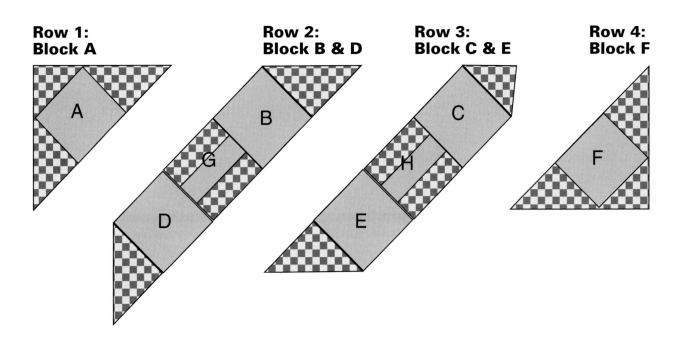

Row 1:
Block A

Row 2:
Block B & D

Row 3:
Block C & E

Row 4:
Block F

Tropical Fruit

In *Tropical Fruit*, you learn how to precisely place embroidery designs and add decorative satin stitching to your embroidered center medallion. This bright and cheery quilt is a welcome addition to any kitchen.

Finished size: 25" x 31"

Embroidery Collections

Amazing Designs Fruit & Veggie Squares Collection I AD1120
Lettering font of your choice

Materials

Fabrics:
    ½ yd. pink fabric
    ½ yd. yellow fabric
    ⅛ yd. magenta fabric
    ⅛ yd. purple fabric
    ⅛ yd. green fabric
    ⅛ yd. blue fabric
    ⅛ yd. orange fabric
    ¼ yd. multi-colored print for binding
    1 yd. backing fabric
1 yd. batting
1 yd. Pellon ShirTailor interfacing
Polymesh cut-away stabilizer

Cutting

blue:
    (4) 4" squares
    (2) 1" x 6¼"
    (2) 1" x 27¼"
pink:
    (1) 6¼" x 20¾"
    (1) 7" x 25"
    (1) 2" x 44"
yellow:
    (1) 6" x 32"
    (1) 2" x 44"
magenta:
    (2) 2" x 44"
purple:
    (2) 2" x 44"
green:
    (8) 1-1½" x 9½"
    (8) 2" x 5¾"
orange border:
    (4) 2¼" strips

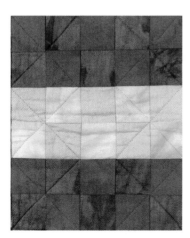

Creating the Checkerboard

1 Sew the yellow and pink 2" x 44" strips together along the long edge.

2 Cut 10 yellow and pink 2" segments.

3 Piece the segments into two strips of five segments each.

4 Sew the magenta and purple 2" x 44" strips together along the long edge.

5 Cut 28 magenta and purple 2" segments.

6 Piece the segments into four strips of five segments and two strips of four segments.

Preparing the Designs

1 Select a font of your choice from an embroidery lettering software program or on your embroidery machine. Two-color fonts work well in this project. The height of the letters should be approximately 85 mm.

2 Print a template of the following letters: F, R, U, I, and T.

3 We're going to alter the fruit and veggie squares by changing the background fill stitch to an appliqué. Open designs #98091, #98077, #98087, and #98084. Delete the first color of all the designs. Save the designs as #98091a, #98077a, #98087a, and #98084a.

#98091 (cherries)

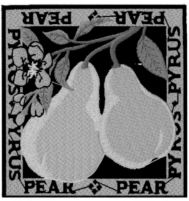

#98077 (pears)

#98087 (watermelon)

#98084 (grapes)

4 Open and Copy (Ctrl C) a scroll design. Paste the scroll into design #98091a. Sit the scroll on top of the fruit square.

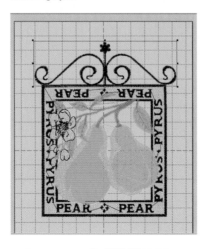

5 Paste the scroll again, select the Mirror Image Vertical tool, and place the second scroll under the fruit square.

6 Repeat for all of the fruit squares. Save the designs as #98091aScroll, #98077aScroll, #98087aScroll, and #98084aScroll.

7 Open design #98084, the grape square. Travel through the design and delete color segments 1, 2, 3, 5, and 6. Save the design as Grapes.

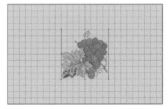

8 Mirror image Grapes horizontally and save it as Grapes MI.

9 Travel through Grapes and Copy (Ctrl C) just the leaf (color segments 4 and 5). Paste (Ctrl V) the leaf into a new file and save it as Leaf.

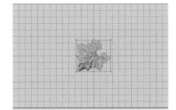

10 Print templates of all the designs.

Embroidering the Fruit Blocks

1 Fuse Pellon ShirTailor interfacing to the wrong side of a 6" x 32" rectangle of yellow fabric.

2 Cut four 6" x 8" rectangles from the interfaced yellow fabric.

3 Tape template #98077aScroll in the center of one rectangle.

4 Load the fabric and polymesh stabilizer in the hoop.

5 Spray the wrong side of one 4" square of blue fabric with temporary adhesive.

6 Place the blue fabric square, tacky side down, in the center of the hoop.

7 Embroider the first color.

8 Remove the hoop from the machine but *Do not remove the fabric from the hoop.*

9 Carefully trim the excess blue appliqué fabric.

10 Place the hoop back on the machine and complete the embroidery design.

11 Repeat for designs #98091aScroll, #98087aScroll, and #98084aScroll.

Adding Satin Stitching

Now the fun part—connecting all of the leaf and grape designs.

1 Draw a curving line with a removable marker to connect the grapes and leaves. Draw from one embroidery design to the next. Travel on top some of the letters. On other sections, stop at the edge of a letter and start up again on the other side of the letter.

2 Set the sewing machine zigzag stitch to SL: 2.0; SW: 0.35.

3 Stitch on the drawn line in a jerky fashion. Twist and turn the fabric as you stitch.

Embroidering the Center Medallion

1 Fuse Pellon ShirTailor interfacing to the wrong side of the rectangle.

2 Tape the font templates in the center of the medallion. Tape the Grapes and Leaf templates as shown. Notice how the grapes and leaves touch a portion of the letters.

3 Once you're satisfied with the composition, replace the templates with miniature crosshairs. Add design names to each crosshair.

4 Load the fabric and polymesh stabilizer in the hoop, centering the F template.

5 Embroider the F.

6 Place the Leaf templates back in the hoop to check the alignment.

7 Move the needle to the center of the Leaf template. Remove the Leaf template and embroider the design.

8 Repeat for the second leaf and remove the block from the hoop.

9 Load the block in the hoop, centering the R template. Embroider the R.

10 Remove the block from the hoop and rehoop, centering the Grape template that overlaps the R.

11 Continue in this fashion until all of the embroidery is completed on the center medallion.

Texas Dusk

The satin-stitched stems on *Texas Dusk* expand the design area of the quilt. Without them, the quilt would be much smaller. What a simple addition to the pretty sunflowers!

Finished Size: 18" x 25"

Embroidery Collection

Designs in Machine Embroidery

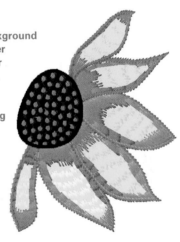

Materials

Fabric:

14" x 21" dark blue for background

1/8 yd. green for inner border

1/4 yd. print for outer border

1/2 yd. backing

1/2 yd. binding

Batting: 18" x 25"

2/3 yd. Pellon ShirTailor interfacing

Polymesh stabilizer

Preparing the Designs

1 Open design #D10002 in your customizing software. Use the Color Select tool to delete color segments one and three. Size the design to 146mm x 71mm. Save the design as Lg3Flowers.

2 Open design #D10004 and delete color segments one and six. Save as #D10004a.

3 Open design #D10010 and delete the first color segment. Save as #D10010a.

4 Open design #D10007 and delete the first color segment. Save as #D10007a.

5 Print templates of Lg3Flowers, #D10004, #D10005, #D10007a, and #D10010a.

Preparing the Fabric

1 Fuse Pellon ShirTailor interfacing to the wrong side of the fabric.

2 Tape the templates on the 14" x 21" blue fabric.

3 Replace the full size templates with miniature crosshairs. To make a miniature crosshair, draw a cross on a piece of tape. Write the design name on the tape. Position the miniature crosshair under the corresponding template.

Lg3Flowers

#D10004

#D10010a

#D10007a

#D10005

Embroidery

1 Place the quilt block in a deep box and spray the wrong side with temporary adhesive.

2 Place polymesh stabilizer on the sticky surface and finger press in place.

3 Hoop the first design area, centering the crosshair in the hoop. Make sure the needle is in the center of the first crosshair. If necessary, move the hoop by touching the editing arrows on the machine screen. Embroider the design.

4 Remove the quilt block from the hoop.

5 Use an iron to remove any hoop marks.

6 Hoop the quilt block, centering the second miniature crosshair. Place the template back in the hoop, aligning the crosshair on the fabric with the template crosshair. Make sure the image on the template will connect with the embroidered design. If necessary, reposition the template. Embroider the design.

7 Repeat for all of the sunflower designs.

8 Embroider the dragonfly design.

9 Place the block, wrong side up, on a pressing surface covered with a terry cloth towel and press.

Adding Satin-Stitched Stems

1 Draw long, slightly curved stems from each sunflower to the lower edge of the quilt. Cross over some of the stems.

2 Set the zigzag stitch at SW: 5.0; SL: 0.35. Sew on the lines.

Finishing

1 Trim the quilt to 13" x 20".

2 Cut the green fabric into 1¾" strips.

3 Sew the inner green border to the quilt top.

4 Cut the outer border fabric into 2½" strips.

5 Sew the outer border strips to the quilt.

6 Layer with batting and backing.

7 Outline quilt around all the embroidery designs.

8 Stitch in the ditch of the borders.

9 Bind as desired.

Providing

a Setting

So far we've looked at fabric as a backdrop for embroidery. Now let's look at fabric as setting the stage for embroidery. The wood fabric in *A Few of My Favorite Things* sets the stage for the everyday items found on the shelves. The grain of the wood runs both vertically and horizontally on the quilt—just like you would find on a piece of furniture. The backs of the shelves appear to be recessed, just as in real life. But, they're not recessed; in fact they are made of the same fabric that's been darkened by black tulle. The valance and footboard are faced so that they appear to be three-dimensional. You can lift the valance since the shaped edge hangs free. All of these techniques set the stage for the embroidery. And, you can do it too.

Later in the chapter we'll look at how appliqué and complementary embroidery designs can set the stage for embroidery.

A Few of My Favorite Things

The success of this quilt is in the replication of the furniture and the variety of embroidery designs used to fill the shelves. I had help from Wendy Etzel's book "The Collectibles Quilt." If you don't have a large selection of embroidery designs for this project, use the ones in your stash and add variety with thread color, mirror imaging, and sizing.

Finished size: 31" x 39"

Embroidery Collections

Amazing Designs Teapot Collection I AD1138
Amazing Designs Cups & Saucers Collection I AD1142
Amazing Designs Country Kitchen Collection I AD1157
Amazing Designs Grandma's Attic Collection I AD1161

Materials

Fabrics:
  2 yd. wood fabric
  34" x 42" backing fabric
  Fabric scraps for books
  ¾ yd. of 72" wide black tulle
Batting: 34" x 42"
1 yd. paper-backed fusible web
Polymesh stabilizer
Transparencies or tracing paper
2 buttons for doorknobs (1")
Teflon protective pressing sheet
Pressing cloth

Cutting Plan

Wood grain running vertically:
  3 panels: 28" x 10"
  2 side moldings: 2½" x 33½"
  2 cabinet doors: 10½" x 10"
  1 book panel: 12" x 10"
Wood grain running horizontally:
  3 shelves: 26¼" x 1¾"
  3 valances: 30½" x 3½"
  1 kickboard: 30½" x 4¼"
  2 facings: 32" x 3"
Black tulle:
  (6) 28" x 10"
  (4) 10½" x 10"
  (1) 12" x 10"

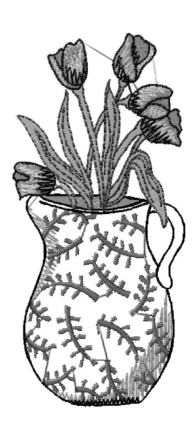

Preparing the Background Fabric

1 Stack two 10½" x 10" layers of tulle on a Teflon protective pressing sheet on a flat surface.

2 Place the fusible web, adhesive side down, on the tulle.

3 Press, following the manufacturer's directions, and remove the paper backing.

4 Place the tulle, adhesive side down, on one 10½" x 10" cabinet door. Cover the tulle with a press cloth and fuse the tulle to the fabric. Some of the adhesive will adhere to the press cloth. Keep

pressing until the adhesive is adhered to the tulle and press cloth. Peel the press cloth off of the tulle.

5 Lower the temperature of the iron to the synthetic setting so that you can iron the tulle without damaging it. Gently touch the hot iron to one corner of the fused tulle. If some residue sticks to the iron, place the press cloth back on the tulle and continue pressing.

6 Repeat for the remaining cabinet door, three 28" x 9" panels, and one 12" x 10" book panel.

7 With a quilters' ruler, chalk a horizontal line 2" from the lower edge of the three 28" x 9" panels.

8 Cover the wrong side of each 28" x 9" panel with tear-away stabilizer.

Preparing the Designs

1 Open design #58149, Amazing Designs Teapot Collection, in your embroidery software. Select the Mirror Image Horizontal tool. Save the design in the appropriate format as #58149MI. Repeat the procedure for design #58096, Amazing Designs Country Kitchen Collection I.

2 Open design #58182, Cups & Saucers Collection. Omit the first color sequence. Save the design as #58182a.

3 Insert tracing paper or transparencies into the printer and print templates of the following designs:

Amazing Designs Teapot Collection I AD1138

#58141 #58149MI

Amazing Designs Cups & Saucers Collection I AD1142

#58119 #58177

Amazing Designs Grandma's Attic Collection I AD1161

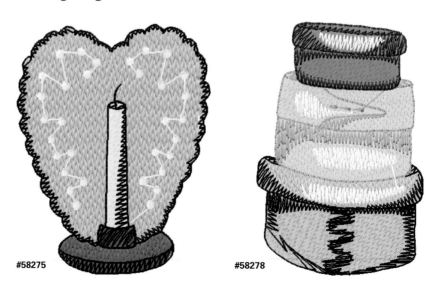

#58275 #58278

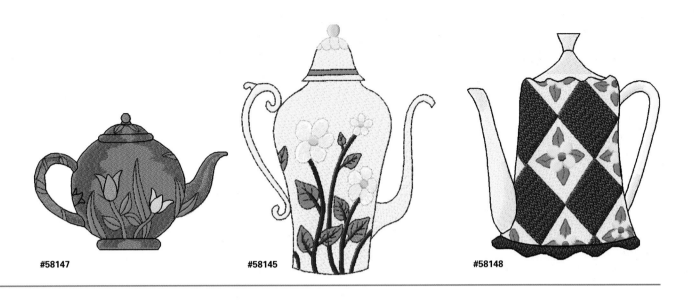

#58147

#58145

#58148

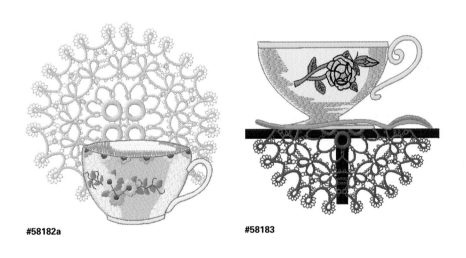

#58182a

#58183

Amazing Designs Country Kitchen Collection I AD1157

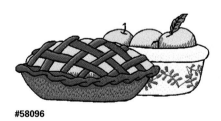

#58096

#58104

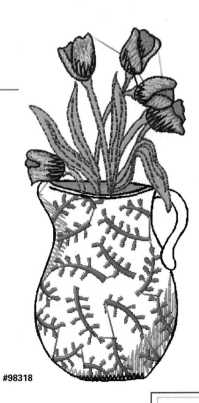

#98318

Embroidery Top Panel

1 Place the teapot template on one of the 28" x 10" panels. Position the template on the chalked line about 5" from the side. Embroider the teapot.

2 Repeat the process for all four teapots, spacing them approximately 6" apart. Set aside.

Embroidery Middle Panel

1 Place template #58177, Cups & Saucers Collection I, in the center of one of the 28" x 10" panels. Position the template on the chalked line. Embroider three identical plates spacing the plates 9" apart.

2 Use template #58119, Cups & Saucers Collection I, to place the stacked cups between the plates. Embroider two stacks.

Embroidery Bottom Panel

1 Use template #58096, Country Kitchen Collection I, to place the first pie on the remaining 28" x 10" panel. Position the template on the chalked line. Embroider the design.

2 Use template #98318, Country Kitchen Collection I, to place the vase of tulips.

3 Use template #58096MI to place the second pie. Use a different thread color for the pie and fruit.

4 Look at template #58104, Country Kitchen Collection I. Notice how the three canisters are not sitting on the same plane. Place the front canister on the chalked line. Embroider the design.

5 Use template #58275, Grandma's Attic Collection I, to place the candle-holder. Embroider the design.

6 Use template #58149MI, Teapot Collection I, to place the teapot. Embroider the design.

7 Use template #58278, Grandma's Attic Collection I, to place the Shaker boxes. Embroider the design. Set aside.

Piecing the Quilt

1 Place a quilters' ruler on the embroidered panel, lining up the bottom edge of the embroidery with the ¼" mark. Cut away the excess fabric.

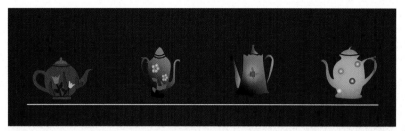

2 Trim the top and middle panels to 26¼" x 6½" and the bottom panel to 26¼" x 7¼".

3 Sew the top panel to a 26¼" x 1¾" shelf. Add the middle panel.

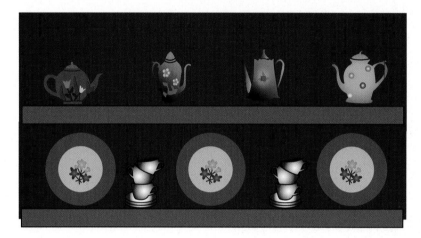

4 Place template #58183, the teacups with lace from Cups and Saucers Collection I, on the top shelf. Make sure the base of the teacup sits directly on the shelf. Embroider a cup between each teapot.

5 Sew the middle panel to another 26¼" x 1¾" shelf and add the bottom panel.

6 Add the bottom shelf to the lower edge.

7 Place template #58182a on an angle under the middle panel shelf. Make sure the cup handle dangles right under the middle shelf. Evenly space and embroider five hanging cups.

Books

1 Cut four 12" strips of novelty fabrics and the wood book panel in varying widths (1½", 1¾", 2", and 2½").

2 Sew the wood fabric to the corresponding novelty fabric along the short edge.

3 Sew the strips together, varying the height of each book.

4 Trim the pieced section to 6" x 10".

 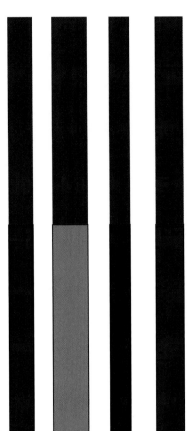 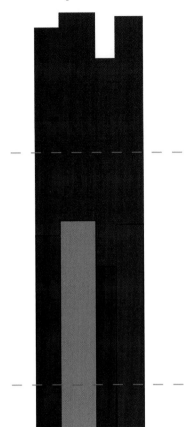

5 Add decorative stitching to the books if desired.

Cabinets

1 Trace two cabinet frames onto the wood fabric from the pattern on page 87.

2 Place the wood fabric and scrap of tulle, right sides together. Sew on the curved line.

3 Turn right-side out.

4 Pin the shaped front on the cabinet front.

5 Select the appliqué stitch and sew on the curved line.

6 Frame the door with 1¾" strips. Repeat for the second cabinet.

7 Piece the book section between the two cabinet doors. Sew the cabinet to the shelf.

Valance and Kickboard

1 To create the three-dimensional valance, trace the valance pattern on page 87 onto one of the valance strips.

2 Sew the two valance strips, right sides together, on the curved line.

3 Trim the seam and turn right-side out.

4 Pin the straight edge to the top of the top shelf. Baste in place.

5 Repeat for the kickboard.

Moldings

1 Sew the two side moldings to the quilt.

2 Attach the upper half of the valance and finish the remaining kickboard seams.

3 Press the quilt top from the wrong side.

Quilting

1 Layer the quilt top with backing fabric and batting.

2 Free-motion quilt the back panels with black thread. All "bare-wood" surfaces were free-motion quilted with light brown thread.

3 Bind the two side edges with wood fabric strips.

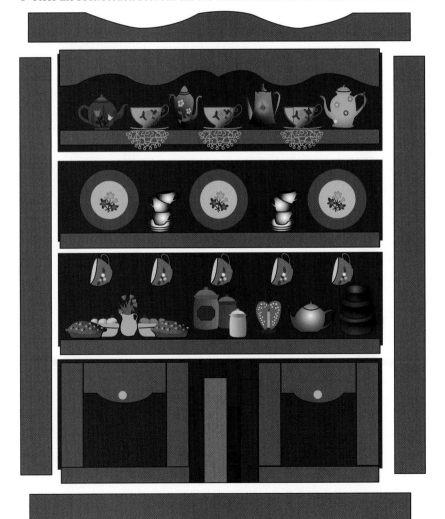

Facings

1 Photocopy the patterns and tape the two sides together to create the full-size appliqué pattern. Trace the upper half of the top valance and the kickboard onto the wrong side of the facing strips.

2 Fold back ¼" on the straight edge and press.

3 Place the shaped sections, right sides together, on the quilt and stitch on the traced lines.

4 Clip all curves. Turn the facings to the wrong side of the quilt and hand sew in place.

5 Sew two buttons to the cabinet doors for doorknobs.

Don't forget to label your quilt!

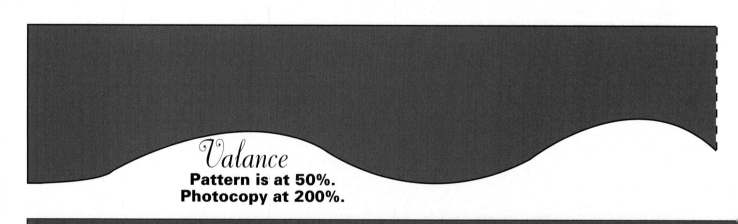

Valance
Pattern is at 50%.
Photocopy at 200%.

Kickboard

Pattern is at 50%.
Photocopy at 200%.

Cupboard Door

**Pattern is at 50%.
Photocopy at
200%.**

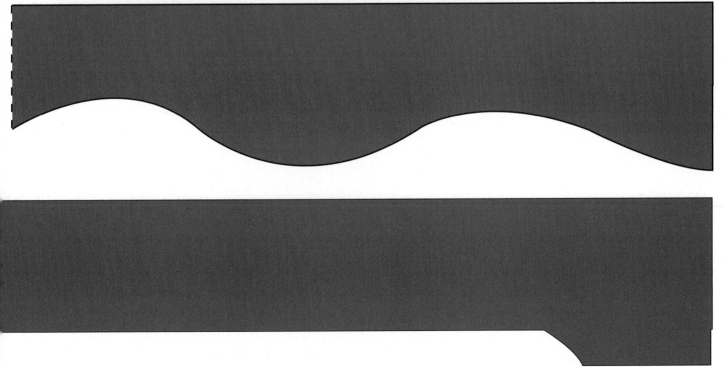

Boo Quilt

Sewing machine appliqué can set the stage for small embroidery designs. The letters B, O, and O provide the perfect resting spot for these small, spooky designs. The appliqué also fills a large vertical space, resulting in a wall hanging that looks at home in any Halloween decor.

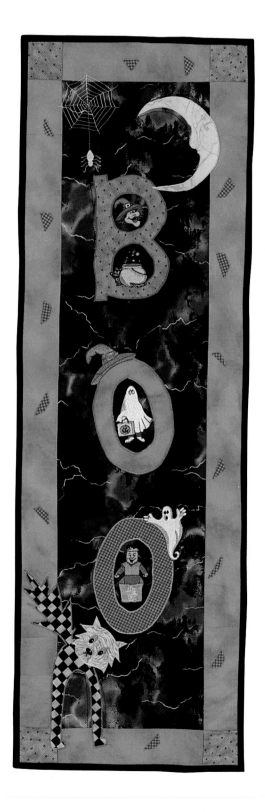

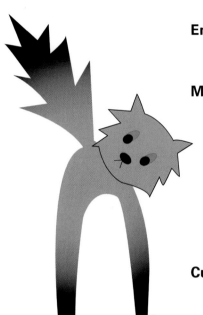

Finished Size: 15 ¼" x 46 ½"

Embroidery Collections

Amazing Designs Fall Holiday Collection I AD1215
Amazing Designs Doll Faces Collection I AD1078

Materials

Fabrics:
  16" x 45" night sky fabric
  ¼ yd. border fabric
  16" x 45" backing fabric
  Scraps for letters, cat, moon and corner stones
  ½ yd. binding
Batting: 16" x 45"
1½ yd. Pellon ShirTailor fusible interfacing
½ yd. paper-backed fusible web
Polymesh stabilizer
Tracing paper or transparencies

Cutting Plan

Border:
(2) 2¾" x 10"
(2) 2¾" x 42"
(4) 2¾" x 2¾"

Preparing the Designs

1 Open design #99627, Fall Holiday Collection I, in Smart Sizer Gold.

2 Click on Color Select and delete colors 1, 2, 3, 4, 5, 6, and 11. Save the design as Hat in the appropriate format.

3 Open design #99629 and resize it to 73.8mm x 93.2mm. Save the design as LgGhost in the appropriate format.

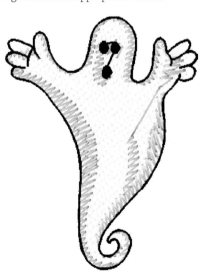

4 Open design #99620 and resize it to 64mm x 95mm.

5 Open design #99621 and resize it to 57mm x 97mm.

6 Open design #99625 and resize it to 95mm x 151mm.

7 Open design #81077, Doll Faces Collection I, and resize to 34mm x 36mm.

8 Save all the resized designs in the appropriate format.

9 Print templates of the following designs:

AD1215 Fall Holiday Collection I
Hat, LgGhost, #99625, #99627, #99623, #99620 and #99621

AD1078 Doll Faces Collection I
#81077

Preparing the Fabric

1 Fuse Pellon ShirTailor interfacing to the wrong side of the background fabric.

2 Trace the BOO letters from the patterns on pages 93-95 onto the paper-backed fusible web.

3 Cut out and fuse the letters B, O, and O to the night sky fabric.

4 Satin stitch the raw edges (SW: 2.0; SL: 0.35).

Embroidery

1 Add polymesh stabilizer to the wrong side of the quilt top.

2 Center and tape template #99627, Fall Holiday Collection I, in the top opening of the letter B. Hoop the quilt and embroider the design.

3 Center and tape template #99623 in the bottom opening of the letter B. Hoop the quilt and embroider the design.

4 Center and tape the Hat template, on the O as shown. Hoop the quilt and embroider the design.

5 Center and tape template #99620 in the center of the O. Hoop the quilt and embroider the design.

6 Center and tape template #99629 on the second O as shown. Hoop the quilt and embroider the design.

7 Center and tape template #99621 in the opening of the second O. Hoop the quilt and embroider the design.

Borders

1 Sew the 2¾" x 42" strips to each side of the quilt.

2 Sew the 2¾" squares to each end of the 2¾" x 10" strips.

3 Pin the short strips to the top and bottom of the quilt matching the seams.

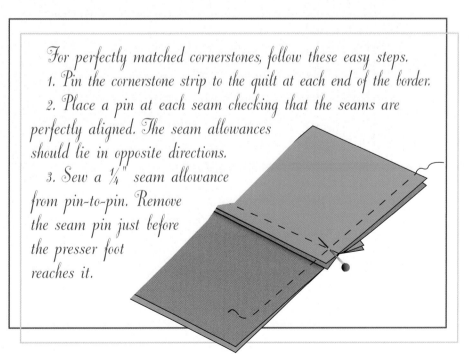

For perfectly matched cornerstones, follow these easy steps.
1. Pin the cornerstone strip to the quilt at each end of the border.
2. Place a pin at each seam checking that the seams are perfectly aligned. The seam allowances should lie in opposite directions.
3. Sew a ¼" seam allowance from pin-to-pin. Remove the seam pin just before the presser foot reaches it.

Cat and Moon Appliqués

1 Trace the cat and moon from the patterns on pages 96-97 onto the fusible web.

2 Cut out and fuse the cat and moon to the quilt top.

3 Satin stitch the raw edges (SW: 2.0; SL: 0.35).

4 Center and tape template #81077, Doll Faces Collection I on the cat's face.

5 Hoop the quilt, centering the cat's face, and embroider the design.

 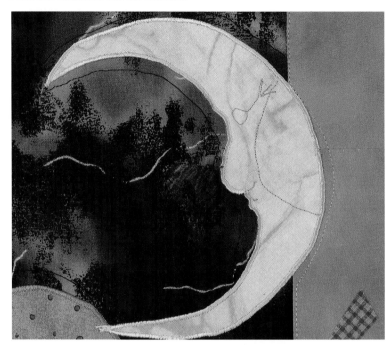

Border Embellishment

1 Fuse paper-backed fusible web to the wrong side of a scrap of orange fabric.

2 Remove the paper backing.

3 Place the quilt on an ironing surface.

4 Hold the fused orange fabric over the quilt and cut irregular shapes. Let the shapes fall on the border, scattering at random.

5 Fuse the scraps in place.

Spider Web

1 Tape template #99625, Fall Holiday Collection I, in the upper right corner of the quilt.

2 Hoop the quilt and embroider the design.

Quilting

1 Layer the quilt with the backing and batting.

2 Outline stitch the letters, cat, moon, and embroidery designs.

3 Stitch in the ditch of the borders.

4 Bind as desired.

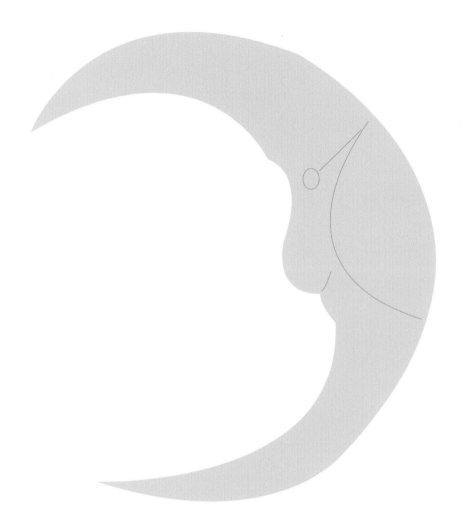

Pattern is at 50%.
Photocopy at 200%.

Butterfly Quilt

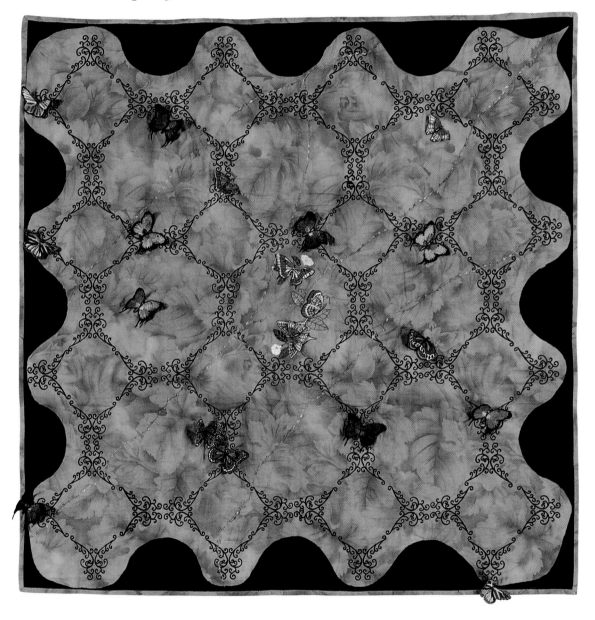

Some embroidery designs are suited to framing other embroidery designs. Notice the filigree design on the *Butterfly Quilt*. It's embroidered four times in a frame-like pattern, similar to a wrought iron gate. The butterflies naturally rest on the gate and fly through the openings.

Finished Size: 43" x 43"

Embroidery Collections

Amazing Designs Fashion Design Collection II AD1045
Amazing Designs Butterfly Collection I AD1014
Amazing Designs Butterfly Collection II AD2008

Materials

Fabrics:
    45" square of muted tones fabric
    45" square of backing
    ⅔ yd. black fabric for border
    ½ yd. black tulle
45" square of thin cotton batting
2½ yd. Pellon ShirTailor interfacing
Polymesh stabilizer
Water-soluble stabilizer

Preparing the Designs

1 Open design #10221, Fashion Design Collection II, in your customizing software. Select a large hoop. Copy (Ctrl C) and Paste (Ctrl V) the design. Reposition it as shown. Color sort the design and save it as #10221a.

#10221

#10221a

Preparing the Fabric

1 Press and starch the 45" quilt top.

2 Fuse the interfacing to the wrong side of the 45" quilt top.

3 Fuse the polymesh stabilizer to the wrong side of the quilt top.

4 Lay the quilt top, wrong side up, on a flat surface. Spray the wrong side of the quilt with temporary adhesive. Finger press the batting onto the tacky surface.

5 Spray the batting with temporary adhesive. Finger press the backing onto the tacky surface.

6 Carefully fold the quilt in half and in half again. Press the folds. Open the quilt to reveal the creases.

7 Center the four #10221a templates on the fabric to create a block.

Embroidering the Wrought Iron Designs

1 Center one of the #10221a templates in the hoop. Roll up the right side of the quilt so you can slide the quilt into the embroidery machine.

2 Move the needle to the center of the template. Remove the template and embroider the design. Remove the fabric from the hoop.

3 Continue to place the templates on the quilt, connecting the image on the template with the previously stitched designs, and embroidering the designs. There are 16 small blocks.

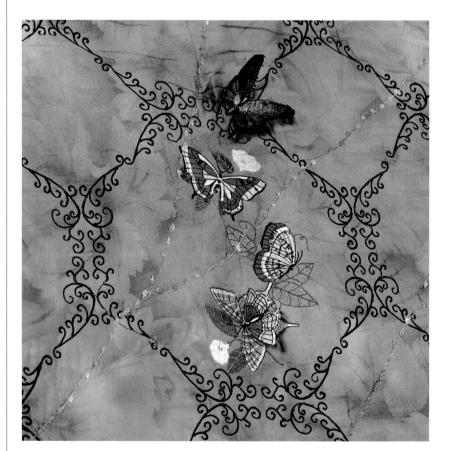

Embroidering the Butterflies

Only three butterflies are stitched on the quilt because I got tired of hooping! The other butterflies were first stitched on tulle and water-soluble stabilizer then tacked to the quilt.

1 Hoop water-soluble stabilizer and two layers of tulle.

2 Place black bobbin thread into the bobbin case.

3 Embroider the butterfly designs.

4 Tear or wash away the water-soluble stabilizer.

5 Trim the tulle close to the embroidery or use a stencil cutter (heated tool) to melt the excess tulle.

6 Randomly tack the butterflies to the quilt (they can cover any misaligned wrought iron designs).

Creating the Scalloped Border

1 Cut the black fabric into four 5" x 45" strips.

2 Spray the wrong side of one strip with temporary adhesive. Finger press the strip to the outside edge of the quilt, overlapping the embroidery designs.

3 Flip the quilt over. Place the quilt in the sewing machine, wrong side up. Sew a curved line, outlining the wrought line embroidery (which is visible on the wrong side of the quilt).

4 On the right side of the quilt, trim away the excess black fabric, revealing the scalloped edge.

5 Satin stitch over the raw edge (SW: 3.5; SL: .035).

6 Repeat on the remaining three sides.

7 Bind the quilt as desired.

Close-up

Scenes

I love wisteria. I love its gnarly branches contrasting strongly with the delicate blooms of each flower. I love how the blooms hang so full and sway in a spring breeze. I love the blushing shades of lilac, pink, and white found on wisteria blossoms. But most of all, I love the arrival of wisteria because the long days of summer are just around the corner.

I designed this collection of embroidery designs so that you could duplicate a branch of wisteria. Just like nature, no two blooms in this collection are alike. You'll find five versions of a wisteria blossom on the CD. And, when stitched in different thread colors and mirror image versions, your wisteria tree will have all the variety of nature's wisteria.

Wisteria Quilt

I love the heavy blooms of wisteria—the way they hang from the branches and sway in the breeze. I also love the gnarly branches, the older the better! This quilt captures those images all year round. All of the embroidery designs for the *Wisteria Quilt* can be found on the CD. There are five wisteria designs, and you can add even more variety by changing the thread colors of each bloom. Some of the leaves are embroidered while others are appliquéd. That same raw edge appliqué technique is used on the trunk and branches and adds a rustic effect. Insert a splash of color into the quilt with the butterflies. Finally, select border fabrics that echo the colors in the quilt.

Finished size: 40" x 39"

Embroidery Collection

Contemporary Machine Embroidered Quilts CD
by Eileen Roche

Materials

Fabrics:
> 45" square of yellow fabric for the background
> 1 yd. brown mottled fabric for tree trunk
> ½ yd. green fabric for the leaves
> ¼ yd. orange fabric for the inner border
> ½ yd. lilac fabric for the outer border
> 42" square of backing fabric
> $^2/_3$ yd. binding

2 yd. paper-backed fusible web
Batting: 42" square
3 yd. Pellon ShirTailor interfacing
Polymesh cut-away stabilizer
Steam-A-Seam 2
Tracing paper

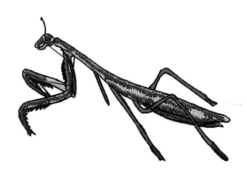

Preparing the Designs

1 Insert the Machine Embroidered Quilts CD by Eileen Roche into the CD-rom drive.

2 Open your customizing software. Go to File, Open and select the CD-rom drive. Select the format appropriate for your machine.

3 Open the following designs and print a template of each design:

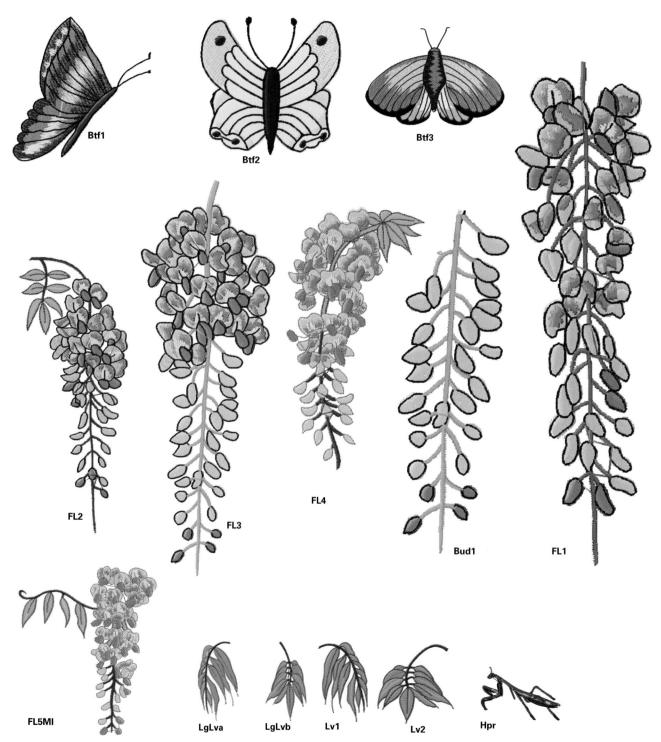

Btf1

Btf2

Btf3

FL2

FL3

FL4

Bud1

FL1

FL5MI

LgLva

LgLvb

Lv1

Lv2

Hpr

Preparing the Fabric

Fuse Pellon ShirTailor interfacing to the wrong side of the entire background.

Appliquéing the Branch

1 Cut a piece of craft paper or newspaper 32" wide x 34" tall. Using the line drawing on page 109 as a guide, freehand draw your own wisteria branch, using the full width and height of the paper. Cut out your pattern and trace it onto paper-backed fusible web.

2 Iron the fusible web to the wrong side of the branch fabric following the manufacturer's directions.

3 Cut out the branch on the traced lines. Use a rotary cutter to access the areas "inside" of the lines. Save the excess fused branch fabric to add additional branches or twigs to the quilt after embroidery.

4 Lay the quilt top on a large, flat pressing surface. Position the branch appliqué on the quilt top. Fuse the branch following the manufacturer's directions.

Cutting the Leaves

There are two methods for cutting the leaves. The first method is just like you used for the branch. The second method encourages you to use your own artistic style and eliminates the tracing step.

Method 1

1 Using the pattern on page 108, trace 130 leaves onto the paper-backed fusible web.

2 Cut out the traced leaf shapes.

3 Remove the paper backing.

Method 2

1 Fuse the paper-backed fusible web to the wrong side of the leaf fabric.

2 Remove the protective paper backing.

3 Use your scissors to cut 130 freeform leaf shapes. It's very simple to do and once you get started, you'll be an expert in no time.

Appliquéing the Leaves

1 Arrange the leaves in clusters. Seven to nine leaves seem to work best. Place the leaves one by one on the quilt, starting with the leaves in the background and working towards the foreground. Tweezers can be helpful when positioning the leaves.

2 Fuse the leaves in place.

3 Save some leaves to add after the embroidery is complete.

Embroidering the Designs

1 Tape the templates of the wisteria blooms on the quilt, referring to the photograph on page 104 for precise placement.

2 Embroider the three blooms on the right first, then begin stitching the blooms in the center area.

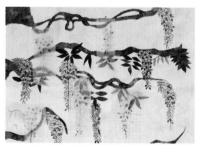

3 As you progress, replace the full size templates with miniature crosshairs. Make sure you mark the crosshair with the design number. Add the initials MI for any designs that need to be mirror imaged.

4 Roll the right side of the quilt and clip it with bicycle clips or large office supply clips.

5 Place polymesh stabilizer behind one of the templates in the center of the quilt.

6 Center the template in the hoop. Embroider the design.

7 Remove the quilt from the hoop. Center the next template, working towards the edge. Continue in this fashion until all of the wisteria blooms are embroidered.

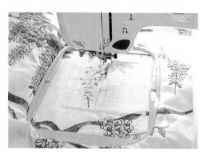

8 Hoop the praying mantis template. Make sure its legs are sitting on the branch. Embroider the design.

9 Embroider the butterflies.

10 To add additional leaves, follow the steps for fusing and appliquéing the leaves. Add some leaf clusters to the top of the wisteria blooms.

Finishing

Now that all of the embroidery is complete, your quilt may not look as flat and square as you'd like. Tips and techniques for whipping it into shape are in Chapter 8. You'll learn how to square the quilt, add borders, quilt, and bind.

Small Wisteria Branch Leaf Pattern

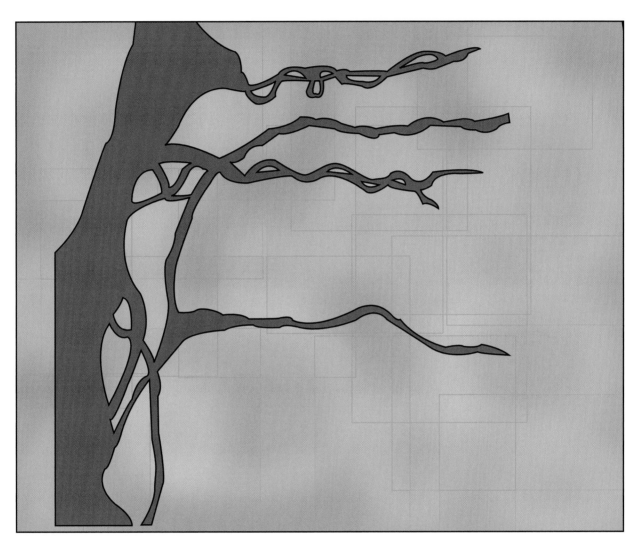

Wisteria Branch

Wisteria Blooms

Try your hand at a simple close-up scene with
Wisteria Blooms. Each block can be embroidered
in a short time, and you'll love the results when
you sew the three blocks together.

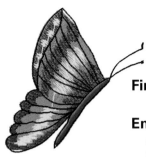

Finished Size: 26½" x 15½"

Embroidery Collection

Contemporary Machine Embroidered Quilts CD
by Eileen Roche

Materials

Fabrics:
    ½ yd. green background fabric
    Fat quarter hot pink fabric
    27" x 16" backing fabric
    ¼ yd. black and white binding
Batting: 27" x 16"
½ yd. paper-backed fusible web
1 yd. Pellon ShirTailor interfacing

Cutting

Green background fabric:
    (3) 10" x 16"
Hot pink sashing fabric:
    (4) 1½" x 14½" strips
    (2) 1½" x 26" strips

Preparing the Designs

1 Insert the Machine Embroidered Quilts CD by Eileen Roche into the CD-rom drive.

2 Open your customizing software. Go to File, Open and select the CD-rom drive. Select the format appropriate for your machine.

3 Open FL2 and FL5. Mirror image each design and save as FL2MI and FL5MI. Open FL2MI and FL5MI and print a template of each design.

Btf1

Btf2

Btf3

FL1

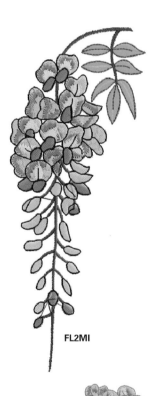

FL2MI

FL4

FL5MI

Hpr

Preparing the Fabric

1 Fuse Pellon ShirTailor interfacing to the wrong side of each green block.

2 Draw an 8" x 14" rectangle in the center of the quilt block with chalk or other removable marker. This is the design area and all appliqué and embroidery will be positioned within this frame.

Note: The appliqué branch patterns will extend beyond the 8" x 14" design area of the block. This ensures that the ends of the appliqués extend beyond the sashing.

Branch Appliqué

1 Fuse fusible web to the wrong side of the branch fabric.

2 Trace the branch designs for Blocks 1, 2, and 3 from the patterns on pages 116-117.

3 Cut the branch patterns for Blocks 1, 2, and 3 on the traced line.

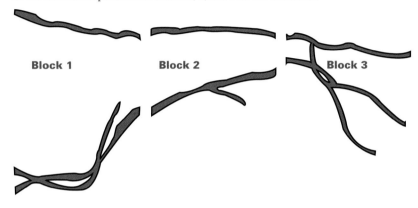

4 Remove the protective paper backing.

5 Lay the quilt blocks on a large, flat pressing surface. Position the branch appliqués on the quilt blocks. Fuse the branches following the manufacturer's directions.

Embroidering Block 1

1 Tape the Hpr template on the branch as shown in the photo.

2 Place poly-mesh stabilizer on the wrong side of the design area.

3 Hoop the quilt block and move the needle to the center of Hpr template. Remove the template and embroider the design. Remove the quilt block from the hoop.

4 Tape the FL2MI template on the quilt block as shown. Make sure the stem of the wisteria blossom is touching the branch.

5 Hoop the quilt block and move the needle to the center of the template. Embroider the design.

6 Remove the quilt block from the hoop.

7 Tape the Btf2 template on the block. Hoop the block, centering the template. Embroider the design.

8 Press the block from the wrong side and set aside.

Embroidering Block 2

1 Tape the FL5MI template on the quilt block as illustrated. Make sure the stem of the wisteria blossom is touching the branch.

2 Place poly-mesh stabilizer on the wrong side of the design area.

3 Hoop the quilt block and move the needle to the center of the template. Embroider the design.

4 Remove the quilt block from the hoop.

5 Tape templates FL1 and BF 1 on the quilt block as illustrated. Make sure the stem of the FL1 is touching the branch. If available, select a 5" x 7" hoop and lay the inner hoop on the quilt block. Check to see if both designs fit in the hoop.

6 Replace one template with a miniature crosshair.

7 Embroider the first design.

8 Move the needle to the center of the miniature crosshair. Remove the miniature crosshair. Embroider the second design.

9 Remove the quilt block from the hoop.

10 Press the block from the wrong side and set aside.

Embroidering Block 3

1 Tape the FL4 template on the quilt block as illustrated. Make sure the stem of the wisteria blossom is touching the branch.

2 Place poly-mesh stabilizer on the wrong side of the design area.

3 Hoop the quilt block and move the needle to the center of the template. Embroider the design.

4 Remove the quilt block from the hoop.

5 Tape two Btf3 templates on the quilt block. Lay the inner hoop of a 5" x 7" hoop on the quilt block. Check to see if the two butterfly designs fit in the hoop.

6 Remove one of the templates and replace it with a miniature crosshair.

7 Embroider the first design.

8 Move the needle to the center of the miniature crosshair. Remove the miniature crosshair. Embroider the second design.

Trimming the Blocks

Trim the embroidered blocks to 8½" x 14½".

Cutting the Leaves

There are two methods for cutting the leaves. The first method is just like you used to cut out the branch. The second method encourages you to use your own artistic style.

Method 1

1 Using the pattern on page 117, trace 40 small wisteria leaves onto the paper-backed fusible web.

2 Cut out the traced leaf shapes.

3 Remove the paper backing.

Method 2

1 Fuse the paper-backed fusible web to the wrong side of the leaf fabric.

2 Remove the protective paper backing.

3 Use your scissors to cut 40 free-form leaf shapes. It's very simple to do and once you get started, you'll be an expert in no time.

Appliquéing the Leaves

1 Arrange the leaves in clusters. Seven to nine leaves seem to work best. Place the leaves one by one on the quilt, starting with the leaves in the background and working towards the foreground. Tweezers can be helpful when positioning the leaves.

2 Fuse the leaves in place.

3 Drop the feed dogs on the machine and attach a free-motion quilting foot.

4 Straight stitch close to the raw edge of the leaves in green and the branches in brown thread.

5 Raise the feed dogs, attach a satin stitch foot and satin stitch the stems of the leaves.

Finishing

1 Sew the blocks to the vertical sashing strips with a ¼" seam allowance.

2 Add the outer border.

3 Layer the quilt top with batting and backing.

4 Quilt in the ditch of all seams. Outline stitch the butterflies and wisteria blooms and stipple the green background areas.

5 Bind as desired.

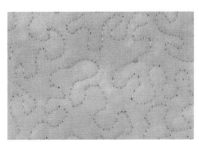

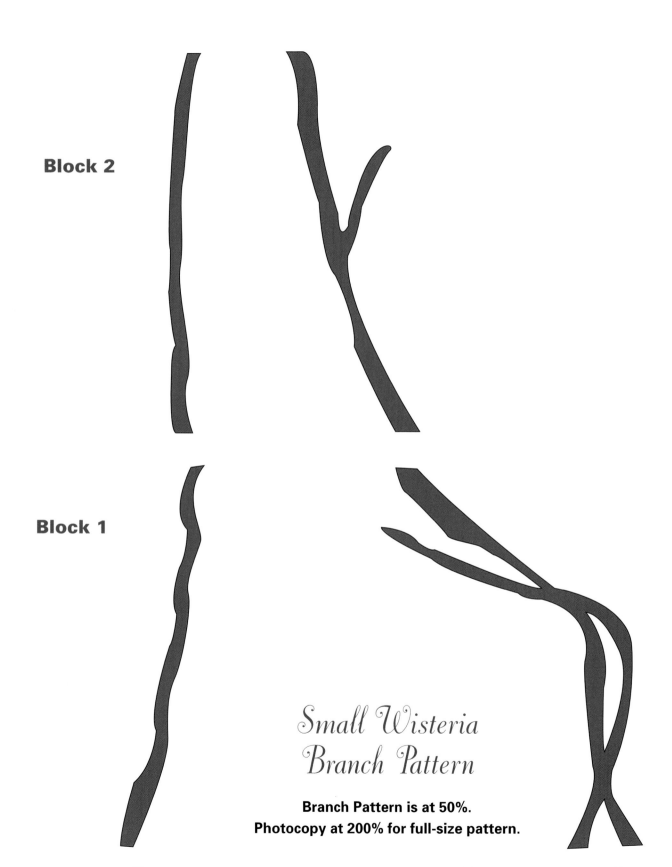

Block 2

Block 1

Small Wisteria
Branch Pattern

Branch Pattern is at 50%.
Photocopy at 200% for full-size pattern.

Block 3

Small Wisteria Branch Pattern

**Branch Pattern is at 50%.
Photocopy at 200% for full-size pattern.**

Small Wisteria Leaves Pattern

Small Wisteria Leaf Pattern

CHAPTER 7

Landscape

Quilts

The very nature of embroidery is time consuming and, often, I want a large finished piece. The solution is sewing machine appliqué. The addition of appliqué pieces helps fill large areas and provides a setting for the embroidery. Although this quilt measures 44" x 45", almost all of the embroidery is located in a 12" x 18" area. The addition of tall blades of appliquéd grass helps enlarge the scene and draws the viewer's eye into the quilt. It also provides you with a large size quilt to hang in a place of honor in your home.

One Silly Frog

The hand-dyed fabrics add a realistic touch to this pond scene. The water lilies are really just two different embroidery designs that were sized and stitched in a variety of colors to add interest. The dragonflies flitting in the sky give motion to an otherwise still scene.

Finished size: 44" x 45"

Embroidery Products

Amazing Designs Floral Collection III AD1004
Amazing Designs Frogs Collection I AD1119
Amazing Designs Dragonflies Collection I AD1173
Amazing Designs Asian Home Decor AD1095

Materials

Fabrics:
  38" x 24" sky fabric
  38" x 11" water fabric
  ½ yd. purple for the inner border and binding
  1½ yd. bamboo fabric for outer border
  ¼ yd. bright green for grass
  ¼ yd. medium green for grass
  48" x 45" backing fabric
Batting: 48" x 45"
Paper-backed fusible web, 2 pieces (10" x 30" each)
Fusible polymesh cut-away stabilizer
4 yds. Pellon ShirTailor interfacing

Preparing the Designs

Water Lilies

1 Open the water lilies designs #84069, (AD 1095 Asian Home Decor) and #44121, (AD 1004 Floral Collection III) in your embroidery software.

2 Mirror image both designs. Save as #84069MI and #44121MI.

3 Click on the Color Select tool in design #84069. Eliminate the first two color segments (the lily pads). Save the design as FL84069.

4 Select design #84069MI and decrease the size to 82mm x 62mm. Save as Sm84069MI.

5 Select design #44121MI and decrease the size to 56mm x 76mm. Save as Sm44121MI.

6 Print three templates of #84069, two of FL84069, one of #84069MI, and one of Sm84069MI.

7 Print three templates of #44121 and one of Sm4421MI.

Dragonflies

Open and print templates of five dragonfly designs (AD 1173 Dragonflies Collection I)

#94510

#94512

#94513

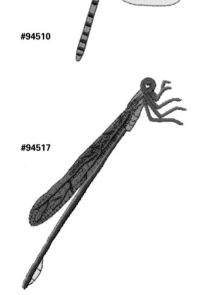

#94517

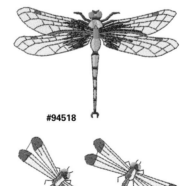

#94518

#94519

Frog

Open design #94006 (AD1119 Frogs Collection I) and print a template.

Preparing the Quilt Top

1 Sew the sky and water together along the long seam. Press the seam allowance toward the water.

2 Fuse Pellon ShirTailor interfacing to the wrong side of the quilt.

3 On the wrong side of the quilt, measure to find the 25" x 30" design area in the center of the quilt top. Lightly outline the area with chalk.

4 Fuse polymesh stabilizer to the wrong side of the design area.

Embroidering the Pond

1 Tape the frog template (#94006) on the horizon. Surround the frog with the water lily templates, working from the background to the foreground. Keep the water lilies within the center design area. Once you are satisfied with the composition, tape the templates securely.

2 Add the dragonfly templates. Tape two dragonflies so that they appear to be eating the flowers. Place the remainder in the sky.

3 Slide a miniature crosshair under each template and label them with the design number and MI, if appropriate

4 Load the stabilized quilt top in the hoop, centering the frog template.

5 Gently roll the right side of the quilt so that you can fit the quilt under the head of the embroidery machine. Use clips to hold the roll in place.

6 Make sure the needle is in the center of the template. Remove the template and embroider the design. Remove the quilt from the hoop.

7 Place the quilt on a pressing surface and press away the hoop marks. Don't let the iron touch any of the miniature crosshairs. They can be difficult to remove and will gunk up the iron!

8 Embroider the water lily designs in a counter clockwise direction, working from the background to the foreground.

9 Tape the corresponding template back on the quilt top, aligning the template with the miniature crosshair. Hoop the stabilized quilt, centering the template. If you have a large hoop, you can embroider more than one design in each hooping, but best results are always achieved by selecting the smallest hoop available for the design.

10 Use a variety of threads to add interest to the lilies and the pads.

11 Continue to press the quilt after each hooping. It is easier to line up the next embroidery design if you're working with flat fabric. Ridges and bumps in the fabric from hoop marks can be permanently captured if not properly removed.

Embroidering the Sky

There are seven dragonfly designs embroidered in the sky. Two of the dragonflies appear to be feeding on the water lilies. The remaining five dragonflies are flitting across the sky.

1 Embroider the dragonflies in a variety of colors. Use a dark gray thread for the final outline to give continuity to the quilt.

2 Two more dragonflies are practically hidden behind the tall grass. Embroider them now.

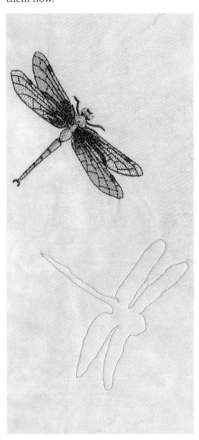

3 The "ghost" dragonflies are not embroidery designs. They were applied in the quilting stage.

Adding Appliqué

Blades of Grass

1 Fuse the paper-backed fusible web to the wrong side of the grass fabrics following the manufacturer's directions.

2 Cut blades of grass in random widths and heights from ¾" to 1½" wide up to 30" tall from the prepared fabric.

3 Remove the paper.

4 Place the quilt top on a large pressing surface. Place the grass strips, adhesive side down, on the quilt top. Fuse the strips onto the quilt, taller blades on the right and left while shorter blades fill in the foreground of the water. Most of the lime green strips are in the foreground. Don't try to achieve perfection, it's only grass!

Finishing

1 Square off the quilt following the instructions in Chapter 8.

2 Add a 2" dark inner border (sample is deep purple) and a 4" outer border.

3 Layer the quilt top with the batting and backing. Use pins or basting stitches to secure it.

4 Free-motion quilt all the exposed edges of the grass.

5 Use yellow thread to add movement to the water.

6 Use monofilament thread to quilt a few dragonfly outlines in the sky. Bind as desired.

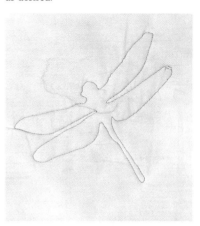

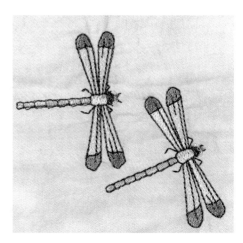

Time for Tea

The inspiration for this tea cozy was the hand-painted fabric. The soft washes of blue were the perfect spot for a pond and creek while the green foreground called for a small garden. The embroidery designs are a unique combination of designs in my stash. You may have similar ones in your stash, too. If you've been collecting birdhouses, then you have a small cottage since the cottage here is really a birdhouse. I just stitched the black opening in gray to match the door and added some free motion quilting stitches to the chimney for smoke.

The flowers in the foreground on the right appear to be very natural, like they've been growing there for quite some time. But, they're half of another embroidery design, a potted plant. They were just the right size and detail for the foreground. I deleted the pots in my software and saved the flowers separately.

Notice the "appliquéd" road. It draws your eye into the scene and tells you that you're viewing a scene, one with distance between the elements. It tells you this through its wide opening in the foreground and its narrow strand in the background. But, it's not really appliqué. I drew the road after all of the embroidery was completed because I hadn't properly planned my project. Once the embroidery was complete, I knew something was missing. So I just drew the road with a brown fabric marker. I liked the technique so much, I enhanced the pond and creek with blue fabric marker. Free-motion quilting adds texture to all of the elements.

Finished Size: 14½" x 11½"

Embroidery Products

Amazing Designs Trees Collection I AD1065
Amazing Designs Birdhouses Collection I AD1091
Amazing Designs Picket Fences Collection I AD1133
Amazing Designs French Country Collection I AD1151

Materials

½ yd. hand-dyed cotton fabric, lining, and batting
Fabric markers: blue and brown
Temporary spray adhesive
½ yd. Pellon ShirTailor interfacing
Tear-away stabilizer

Preparing the Designs

1 Print a template of designs #89056 and #89067 from Birdhouses Collection I.

#89056 (cottage)

#89067 (birdhouses)

2 Print a template of designs #44281, #44285, and #64197, Trees Collection I.

#44281 (trees)

#64197 (tree)

#44285 (tree)

3 Print a template of designs #98259 and #98266, Picket Fences Collection I.

#98259 (bridge)

#98266 (arch)

4 Open designs #98279 and #98271, French Country Collection I, in customizing software.

5 Delete the color segments that stitch the pots. Save the designs as #98279a and #98171a. Print a template of both designs.

#98279 (yellow flowers in pot)

#98279a (yellow flowers without pot)

#98171 (mixed flowers in pot)

#98171a (mixed flowers without pot)

Preparing the Fabric

1 Fuse Pellon ShirTailor interfacing to the wrong side of the hand painted fabric.

2 Trace two (one front, one back) of the tea cozy pattern onto the hand painted fabric, lining and batting.

3 Cut out one of the patterns and set it aside.

4 Place the templates on the traced pattern creating a realistic landscape.

5 Sketch in the road and creek.

6 Once you're satisfied with the composition, add miniature crosshairs with design names under the corresponding templates. Remove the templates.

Embroidering the Designs

1 Hoop the fabric and stabilizer, centering a template in the background. Embroider all of the designs in the background first. Then work toward the foreground.

2 Remove the fabric from the hoop and repeat the process until all the embroidery is completed.

Drawing the Creek and Road

Using fabric markers, draw the road, pond, and creek.

Quilting the Tea Cozy

1 Spray the batting with temporary adhesive and finger press the embroidered fabric to the batting.

2 Free-motion quilt small curving shapes in the road making the shapes smaller and closer together as you move toward the cottage.

3 Free-motion quilt some blades of grass along the edge of the road, pond, creek, and around the base of the cottage and tree.

4 Free-motion quilt the creek.

Constructing the Tea Cozy

1 Cut out the embroidered front section on the traced line.

2 Spray the second piece of batting with temporary adhesive and finger press the tea cozy back to the batting.

3 Stipple the back section.

4 Cut a 6" x 2" strip of fabric. Fold in half lengthwise, press, turn the edges into the center, fold, press again, and topstitch in place.

5 Fold the strip in half crosswise and pin it to the top of the tea cozy front. Baste it to the front.

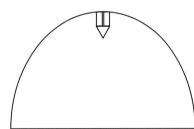

6 Place the front and back sections, right sides together, and sew with a ½" seam allowance, catching the fabric strip and leaving the bottom open for turning.

7 Turn a ½" hem on the lower edge and press. Turn right-side out.

8 Cut two of the pattern from the lining fabric.

9 Place the front and back lining sections, right sides together, and sew with a ½" seam allowance, catching the fabric strip and leaving the bottom open for turning.

10 Turn a ¾" hem on the lower edge of the lining and press.

11 Slip the lining inside the tea cozy wrong sides together, matching the side seams. Topstitch the lower edge.

Tea Cozy Pattern

**Shown at 25%.
Photocopy at 400%.**

Quilting

CHAPTER 8

Wisteria Blooms
Eileen Roche
Flower Mound, TX
February, 2004

Essentials

Now that all the embroidery is
complete, it's time to turn your
masterpiece into a quilt. Your masterpiece
may not look so perfect right now. It may
have lost its square edges and is having
trouble laying flat. Not to worry,
I have some tips to help you
finish.

After applying all that embroidery to your quilt top, the quilt no longer resembles a square. The square is what you started with and the shape inside is what it looks like now. If you want your wall hanging to hang flat, you have to square off the edges.

1 Note the new shape of the quilt in the image above.

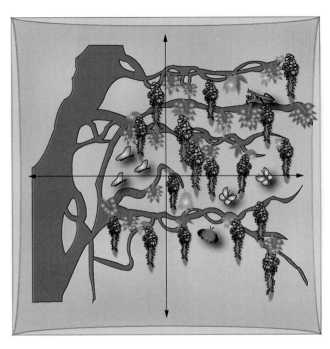

2 Measure the center of the quilt, horizontally and vertically.

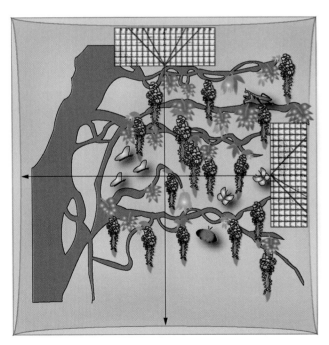

3 Place two quilters' rulers on the quilt as shown.

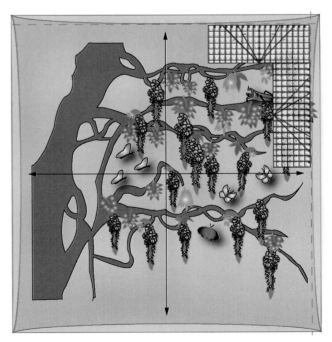

4 Chalk a line on the edge of both rulers. Move the rulers to create a corner.

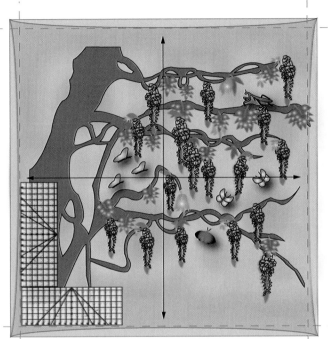

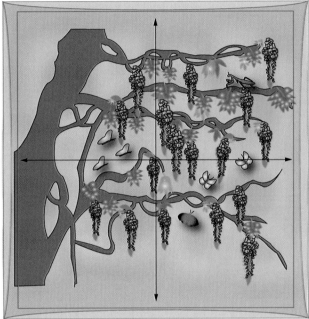

5 Now, move the rulers to the next corner and chalk new lines, connecting the previously drawn lines.

6 Repeat for all four corners until you have drawn a new square.

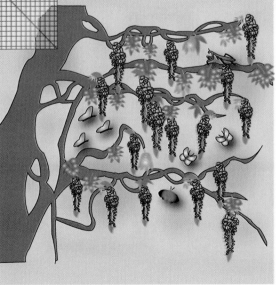

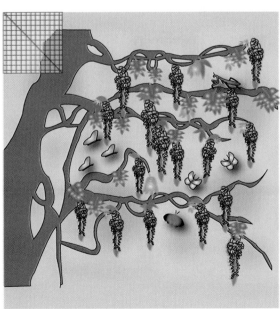

7 Now, check your measurements. Measure the vertical and horizontal centers as shown in step 2. Measure the outside edges. Cut the quilt top on the chalked lines.

8 Check the corners by placing a ruler on each corner.

Borders are a very personal choice, but there are a few guidelines to follow. The main function of the borders is to "frame" the artwork, just like a painting. Therefore, the borders need to draw the viewer into the scene. The borders can also help move the eye around the quilt.

Without the orange border, the eye spots the orange butterfly and stops at the butterfly.

The orange inner border on *Wisteria* helps draw the eye around the whole quilt.

When creating *The Haunting Graveyard*, I found the opposite to be true. I had completed all of the appliqué and embroidery on *The Haunting Graveyard* and couldn't wait to add the funky, striped border. After its addition, I realized the border fabric completely dominated the scene. The dark background fabric, appliqué, and embroidery simply vanished when placed next to the bold, colorful border fabric. The addition of one more design, the stacked pumpkins in the front and center, was the solution. The colorful embroidery design helps pull the eye from the border and into the scene. The eye then travels up the appliquéd road towards the embroidery in the distance.

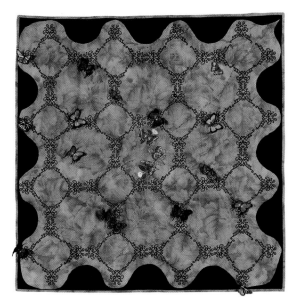

The free-form scalloped border on the *Butterfly Quilt* echoes the scroll pattern of the embroidered wrought iron.

The starting point for *One Silly Frog* was the batik bamboo fabric. Although I felt it was perfect for a border, I knew it would also have to be toned down with a simple, solid block of color. *One Silly Frog* is a busy, landscape scene. The viewer's eye is drawn into the scene by the tall appliquéd grasses on both sides. All of the embroidery is located in the center of the quilt. The bamboo batik fabric reinforces the tropical feel and adds a whimsical touch to the scene.

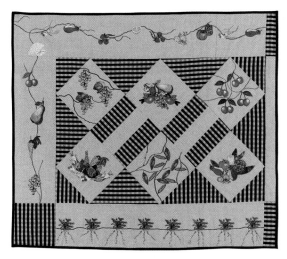

Embroidery can also function as a border. Here, *Nature's Bounty* is bordered on three sides in an asymmetrical fashion. Notice how satin stitching connects all the embroidery designs in the three borders. The satin stitching helps create a linear element, which moves the eye around the quilt.

To Miter or Not to Miter

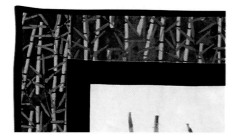

I leave the mitering decision up to the fabric. For instance, the batik bamboo border is not mitered because the vertical print is more effective when left alone on the vertical edges.

Both borders on the *Wisteria* quilt are mitered because it's a professional finish for fabrics without a directional print.

Mitering Borders

1 Measure your quilt.

2 Cut the inner and outer borders about 8" longer than the quilt measurements.

3 Sew the inner and outer borders together along the long edges.

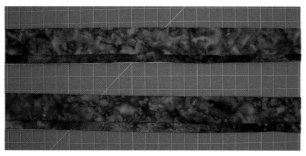

4 Mark ¼" from each corner on all sides of the quilt.

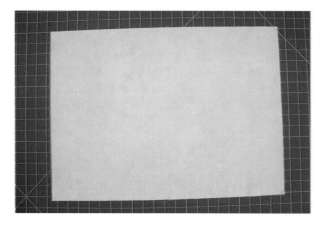

5 Pin the borders to the top, bottom, and sides of the quilt, right sides together.

6 Stitch from each ¼" mark as illustrated.

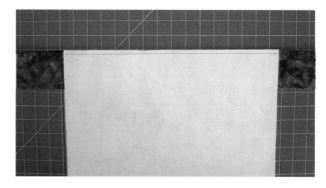

7 Repeat for the remaining three sides, making sure to stop ¼" from each corner and leaving about 4" extra on each border strip.

8 Press the borders from the right side of the quilt.

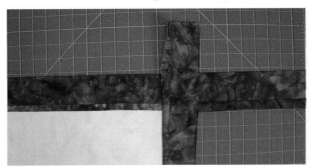

9 Lay one of the borders flat. Fold the adjacent border, forming a miter. Align the two outer edges of the borders.

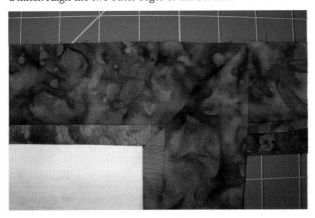

10 Press the mitered corner. Pin the borders on the creased fold.

11 Stitch on the crease, sewing to the outer edge.

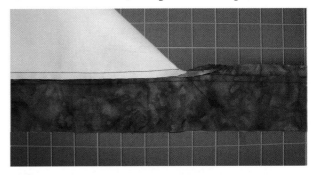

12 Use a quilters' ruler to check for accuracy.

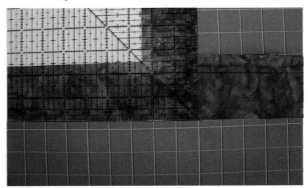

13 Trim the seam allowances and press the seam open.

Now it's time to turn your embroidered masterpiece into a quilt.

1 Cut the backing fabric about 3" larger than the quilt top on all sides.

2 Cut the batting about 1" larger than the quilt top on all sides.

3 Press the backing fabric to remove all folds and creases.

4 Tape the backing fabric right-side down to a flat surface such as a cutting table, dining room table, or floor. Tape one side then gently tug on the fabric before taping the opposite side. Repeat for the top and bottom of the quilt.

5 Spray the fabric with temporary adhesive.

6 Finger press the batting on the backing, smoothing the batting from the middle towards the edges.

7 Spray the batting with temporary adhesive.

8 Smooth the quilt top on the batting, smoothing the quilt top from the middle towards the edges.

9 Make sure the quilt top is centered on the batting and backing. Both the backing and batting should be visible around the perimeter of the quilt.

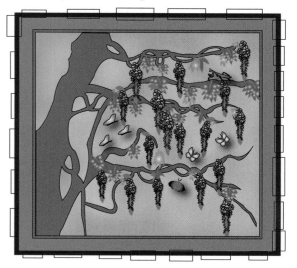

10 Pin baste the quilt with quilters' safety pins, spacing the pins about 3" apart. Don't pin through the embroidery designs, it's best to pin around the embroidery.

Usually the label is the last thing you add to a quilt, but lately I've been adding the label to the quilt right before I stipple. I pin the label to the wrong side and stipple from the right side, catching the label in my stitches. This way it is permanently attached and can be removed only by removing the quilting stitches.

Handwritten Labels

To create a handwritten label, follow these easy steps:

1 Press under all edges on a 4" x 6" rectangle of light-colored fabric.

2 Write your name, address, phone number, date, and name of the quilt in permanent marker. Add some fabric scraps from the quilt.

Embroidered Labels

1 Open your lettering software on your computer.

2 Select a 5" x 7" hoop (if your machine can accommodate one).

3 Enter your name, address, phone number, date, and name of the quilt. If you'd like, add one of the embroidery designs from the quilt.

4 Hoop the fabric and stabilizer (such as polymesh cut-away).

5 Embroider the text and design.

6 Remove the fabric from the hoop and trim it to a manageable size (5" x 7").

Adding the Label to the Quilt

1 From the right side of the quilt, find a spot without embroidery and pin the label to that area on the wrong side.

2 When you quilt that area, you'll catch the label, securing it permanently to the quilt.

There are several options for setting up your machine for quilting. The machine should sit on a table or cabinet that has a large, flat work surface. I have three different work areas that I use for quilting.

1. At home, the machine sits in a cabinet.

2. Also at home, I use the dining room table for larger quilts and add a table extension on the machine.

3. In my office sewing room, I place the machine with the table extension on the cutting table and stand when I quilt. Standing gives me a great view of the quilt while I'm quilting and helps me relax my shoulders and upper body. It also makes it easy to stop and answer the phone!

Free Motion Quilting

Most of the quilting on my embroidered quilts is stippling, a free form meandering stitch. Often I outline an embroidery design to emphasize its shape, then stipple right up to the edge of the outline. My stippling style is small puzzle piece shapes; yours may be entirely different and will become your own quilting signature.

1 Lower the feed dogs on the machine.

2 Attach a darning or embroidery foot.

3 Look at the quilt and make a plan beginning in the center of the quilt.

4 Roll the quilt so you can fit it under the head of the sewing machine and secure it with bicycle or bulldog clips.

5 Wear cotton quilters' gloves to hold the quilt. Place your hands flat on the quilt about 8" apart.

6 If your machine has a speed control feature, set it for medium high. Then hit the gas! If the speed is set, you can push the pedal to the floor while maintaining an even speed. If not, you'll have to find the right speed and keep your foot in that position. With the speed engaged, start moving your hands in a gentle, curving motion. It takes a little practice, but in no time your stitches will be even. I've always said, if you can drive, you can stipple. I find it very similar to driving on a curvy, country road.

7 When you come to a safety pin, leave the needle in the down position and remove the pin.

8 Reroll the quilt when you finish stitching in one area.

9 Feel free to quilt different shapes in different areas, but remember to keep the density of stitching the same throughout the quilt.

On Wisteria, I free-motion quilted the entire tree branch appliqué first. I started in the center of the quilt and stitched close to the raw edge of the appliqué, securing the appliqué, the quilt, batting, and backing all in one step. Next, I stippled the background fabric in a pale yellow thread. Last, I stitched the edges of the appliqué leaves and added the satin-stitched veins.

Quilting the Borders

Stitch in the ditch on the seam between the quilt and the inner border and the seam between the inner and outer borders.

1 Raise the feed dogs.

2 Attach an even feed foot.

3 Set the stitch length for 2.2.

4 Match the thread to the border fabric.

5 Sew parallel lines, ½" apart, stopping at the miters with the needle down to turn the corners. Or you may choose to stipple in the border.

Adding the binding is the last step in finishing your quilt.

1 Trim the excess batting and backing.

2 Mark ¼" from each corner on all sides.

3 Cut strips 2¾" on the straight grain.

4 Sew the strips on the bias.

5 Fold back ¼" on one short end and press.

6 Press the binding strip in half, wrong sides together.

7 Place the binding strip right sides together on the quilt top, starting in the middle of one edge of the quilt. Sew with a ¼" seam allowance.

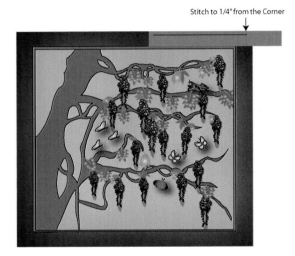

Stitch to 1/4" from the Corner

8 Stop stitching at the ¼" mark before the corner with the needle in the down position. Lift the presser, pivot the quilt, and stitch to the corner.

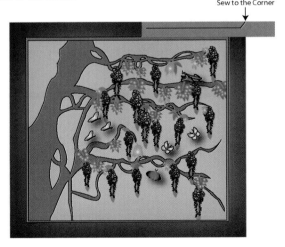

Sew to the Corner

9 Remove the quilt from the machine and fold the binding up, creating a 45-degree angle as illustrated.

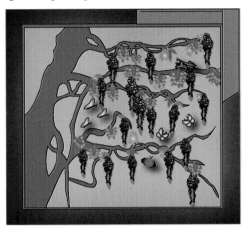

10 Fold down the binding, aligning the fold with the top edge of the quilt and the raw edge of the binding with the side edge of the quilt. Sew from the marked point. Repeat for all corners.

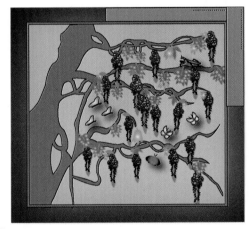

11 When you get to the starting point, insert the binding into the folded edge and trim any excess.

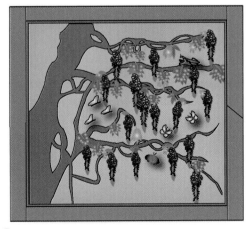

12 Press the binding to the wrong side and pin. Hand-stitch the binding to the backing.

If you plan to use your quilt as a wall hanging, a sleeve is an important addition.

1 Cut an 8" strip of backing fabric, 1" shorter than the width of the quilt.

2 Fold in half, wrong sides together, and sew a ¼" seam lengthwise.

3 Turn right-side out and press.

4 Pin the sleeve on the quilt back, just under the binding and hand-stitch the sleeve to the quilt.

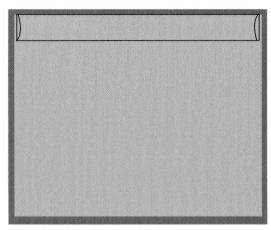

5 Fold up ½" at the top of the sleeve. Pin the lower edge and hand-stitch the sleeve to the quilt. This extra ½" of fabric will allow the quilt to lay flat against the wall.

Resources

Embroidery Designs

Amazing Designs
www.amazingdesigns.com

Cactus Punch
www.cactuspunch.com

Creative Design
www.creativedesigndirect.com

Criswell
www.k-lace.com

Designs in Machine Embroidery
www.dzgns.com

Embroideryarts
www.embroideryarts.com

Embroidery Central
www.embroidery.com

Embroidery Library
www.emblibrary.com

Martha Pullen
www.marthapullen.com

OESD
www.embroideryonline.com

Vermillion Stitchery
www.vsccs.com

Embroidery Machines

Baby Lock
www.babylock.com

Bernina
www.berninausa.com

Brother International Corporation
www.brothersews.com

Janome
www.janome.com

Pfaff
www.pfaffusa.com

Singer
www.singerco.com

Viking
www.husqvarnaviking.com

Software

Amazing Designs

Brother

Bernina

Baby Lock

Buzz Tools®
www.buzztools.com

Drawings®
www.stitchtree.com

Generations
www.generationsemb.com

Husqvarna/Viking

OESD

Origins
www.orginssoftware.com

Pfaff

Singer

Thread

Coats & Clark
www.coatsandclark.com

Madeira®
www.madeirausa.com

Mettler
www.mettler.com

Robison-Anton
www.robison-anton.com

Sulky
www.sulky.com

Stabilizers/ Interfacing

Hoop-It-All
www.hoopitall.com

HTC Products
www.htcproducts.net

OESD

Pellon
www.pellonideas.com

Sulky
www.sulky.com

Viking

Supplies

Nancy's Notions
www.nancynotions.com

Embroider This
www.embroiderthis.com

Magazines

Creative Machine Embroidery
www.cmemag.com
1-800-677-5212

Designs in Machine Embroidery
(Eileen Roche)
www.dzgns.com
1-888-739-0555

Sew Beautiful
www.marthapullen.com
1-800-547-4176

Sew News
www.sewnews.com
1-800-289-6397

Threads
www.threadsmagazine.com
1-800-888-8286

Books

KP Books
www.krause.com
1-800-258-0929

About the Author

In 1995, Eileen Roche was embroidering on sweatshirts, towels, and totebags. Quickly, she became bored. She loves fabric, thread, and texture and yearned to combine all three with embroidery. Quilting offered a new canvas with an endless array of possibilities. Eileen began combining novelty fabrics, hand-painted treasures, and highly textured textiles with embroidery designs and loved the results (well, almost all of the results). She learned that her limited drawing skills were not a liability. In fact, the embroidery designs handled all the details. She began building around embroidery designs by adding larger appliqués and decorative stitches. When she noticed how much fun she was having making embroidered quilts, she thought you would like to learn, too.

Although Eileen is considered an expert on machine embroidery, this is her first book! Eileen is founder and editor of *Designs in Machine Embroidery* magazine and a frequent guest on PBS television shows, *Sewing With Nancy®*, *Martha's Sewing Room®* and the *Linda MacPhee Workshop*. In addition, Eileen has designed embroidery collections for Amazing Designs and *Designs in Machine Embroidery*. She has taught at industry trade shows across the United States reaching thousands of machine embroidery enthusiasts.

Currently a resident of Flower Mound, Texas, Eileen started *Designs* magazine in 1998 in Morton, Pa. as a machine-specific newsletter. Since that time, she has transformed *Designs* into the industry's leading source of inspiration for the home embroidery enthusiast.

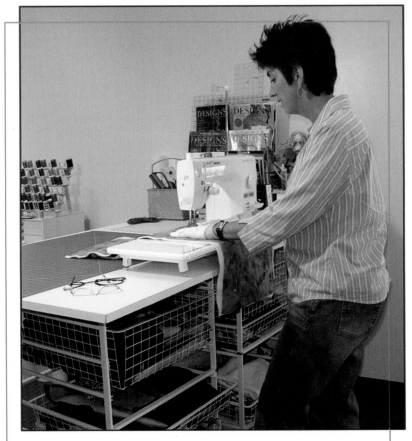